Cascading Style Sheets 2.0

PROGRAMMER'S REFERENCE

Eric A. Meyer

Osborne/**McGraw-Hill**

New York   Chicago   San Francisco
Lisbon   London   Madrid   Mexico City   Milan
New Delhi   San Juan   Seoul   Singapore   Sydney   Toronto

Osborne/**McGraw-Hill**
2600 Tenth Street
Berkeley, California 94710
U.S.A.

To arrange bulk purchase discounts for sales promotions, premiums, or
fund-raisers, please contact Osborne/**McGraw-Hill** at the above address.
For information on translations or book distributors outside the U.S.A.,
please see the International Contact Information page immediately
following the index of this book.

Cascading Style Sheets 2.0 Programmer's Reference

1234567890 DOC DOC 01987654321

ISBN 0-07-213178-0

Publisher   Brandon A. Nordin
Vice President & Associate Publisher   Scott Rogers
Acquisitions Editor   Jim Schachterle
Project Editor   Madhu Prasher
Acquisitions Coordinator   Tim Madrid
Copy Editor   Mike McGee
Proofreader   Paul Tyler
Indexer   Claire Splan
Computer Designers   Tara Davis and Lucie Ericksen
Illustrator   Michael Mueller
Series Design   Peter F. Hancik

This book was composed with Corel VENTURA™ Publisher.

To my wife, Kathryn, and a secluded dance
under a starry California sky

About the Author

Eric A. Meyer has been working with the Web since late 1993. After six years as campus Webmaster at Case Western Reserve University, he joined The OPAL Group (www.theopalgroup.com), an information technology consulting firm in Cleveland, Ohio, which is a much nicer city than you might have heard. Eric is an invited expert with the W3C's CSS Working Group, and coordinated the creation of the CSS Test Suite for the W3C (www.w3.org). As of this writing, he is author of three highly popular HTML tutorials, three books, and dozens of articles on CSS and Web design. Eric also teaches CSS classes online and gives talks at various conferences and seminars. Anyone with an ear for early 20th-century swing and jazz is invited to check out his show, "Your Father's Oldsmobile," which is heard weekly on WRUW 91.1-FM in Cleveland (www.wruw.org). When not otherwise busy, Eric is usually bothering his wife Kathryn in some fashion.

CONTENTS @ A GLANCE

CONTENTS

viii Contents

Contents   ix

x Contents

II   Summaries

INTRODUCTION

In the beginning, there was HTML. And it was pretty good, but not great. You couldn't really create nifty visual designs with it, which gave rise to table-based layout and single-pixel GIF tricks. And that was pretty bad. So CSS was born, and it was very good—in theory, anyway. There was a long struggle to make CSS a viable technology, thanks to imperfect interpretations of the specification, but lo! The day arrived when CSS could be used without fear and dread. And the people rejoiced.

Thanks to CSS, designers can cut back on the FONT and table tricks they've been forced to cobble together, and dramatically clean up their markup. With the coming of XHTML and XML, both of which are deeply semantic and must rely on some styling mechanism to become visually appealing, CSS is growing more and more popular. It's a flexible, easy-to-understand language which offers designers a lot of power. Because it reduces markup clutter, it makes pages easier to maintain. And its centralized styling abilities lets designers adjust page layout with quick, easy edits of the styles, not dramatic changes to the markup. In fact, CSS makes it possible to completely reshape the look of a document without changing a single character inside the BODY element.

This book endeavors to efficiently describe the properties and values of CSS2, which was the latest CSS standard when the book was written, and to provide details on property interactions, common authoring mistakes, and other information which designers should find useful.

The text has been arranged to present basic concepts first, with details on important CSS algorithms and behaviors (Chapter 1). This is followed with "core" information which describes the types of values that can be used in CSS2 (Chapter 2), and the various ways in which elements can be selected for styling (Chapter 3). This first part of the book does its best to describe the foundation of CSS, for the rest of it would not function without the values and concepts presented.

The middle of the book (Chapters 4 through 6) is the largest portion, and is probably the area where readers will spend the most time—all of the properties found in CSS2 are defined, described, and annotated with notes. These properties are broken up into separate chapters, with Chapter 4 devoted to visual-media properties, Chapter 5 to paged-media properties, and Chapter 6 to aural-media properties. Each property is described in terms of its allowed values, its initial (or default) value, and other common aspects. There are also detailed descriptions of the meaning of each allowed value, notes about how the property works, examples of the property in use, and a list of related properties.

The final part of the book (Chapters 7 through 9) contains other useful information about CSS, including a browser support chart, a CSS2 property quick reference, and a list of useful online resources. Between the contents of this book and the resources provided, it should be possible to decipher any CSS conundrums you may encounter. Although CSS can sometimes seem a bit mystifying, it is more than worth the effort of learning its secrets. Enjoy!

Part I
Reference

Chapter 1
Basic CSS Concepts

In order to comprehend how CSS affects the presentation of a document, there are some key concepts that must be grasped. Once these are understood, even in part, it becomes easier to see how the properties and values of CSS work. Do not, however, feel that you must completely understand everything in this chapter before experimenting with CSS. In fact, it is better to review this chapter first, then refer back to it as properties are used.

Associating Styles with Documents

There are four ways to associate styles with a document. These range from associating a separate stylesheet with your document to embedding style information in the document itself.

LINK Element

The `LINK` element is found in HTML and XHTML, and is used to associate an external stylesheet with a document.

Generic Syntax
```
<link rel="..." type="text/css" href="..." media="...">
```

Attributes

rel="..."
This attribute describes the relation of the LINKed file to the document itself. For external stylesheets, there are two possible values: `stylesheet` and `alternate stylesheet`. Any `LINK` with a `rel` of `stylesheet` will be used in the styling of the document. The value `alternate stylesheet` is used to refer to stylesheets that are not used in the default rendering of the document, but which can, in theory, be selected by the user and thus change the presentation. The user agent must provide a mechanism to do so in

order for this to work, and unfortunately most user agents do not provide such a mechanism. This attribute is *required*.

href="..."
The value of this attribute is the URL of the external stylesheet. Either relative or absolute URLs may be used. This attribute is *required*.

type="text/css"
This is used to declare the type of data which is being LINKed to the document. When associating a CSS stylesheet, the only allowed value is `text/css`. Other stylesheet languages will call for different values (e.g., `text/xsl`). This attribute is *required*.

media="..."
Using this attribute, one can declare a stylesheet to apply only to certain media. The default value is `all`, which means that the styles will be used in all media in which the document is presented. Recognized values under CSS are `all`, `screen`, `print`, `projection`, `aural`, `braille`, `embossed`, `handheld`, `tty`, and `tv`. Any number of these values can be used in a `media` attribute by formatting them as a comma-separated list. This attribute is optional.

Notes

In this approach, the stylesheet is placed in its own file. Such files are usually given an extension of `.css`, such as `main-styles.css`. The `LINK` element must be placed inside the `HEAD` element in HTML and XHTML, but XML-based markup languages may have other requirements.

Examples

```
<link rel="stylesheet" type="text/css"
   href="http://www.my.site/styles/basic.css">
<link rel="stylesheet" type="text/css" href="article.css"
   media="screen,projection">
<link rel="stylesheet" type="text/css" href="printout.css"
   media="print">
```

STYLE Element

The `STYLE` element is found in HTML and XHTML, and is used as a container for an embedded stylesheet.

Generic Syntax

```
<style type="text/css" media="...">
```

Attributes

type="text/css"
This attribute is handled the same as that used on the LINK element. This attribute is *required*.

media="..."
This attribute is handled the same as that used on the LINK element. This attribute is optional.

Notes
STYLE must be placed in the HEAD element under HTML and XHTML.

Examples

```
<style type="text/css">
H1 {color: purple; border-bottom: 1px solid maroon;}
H2 {color: blue; background: cyan;}
</style>
<style type="text/css" media="all">
PRE, CODE, TT {font-family: monospace; color: #333;}
PRE {margin-left: 3em;}
</style>
```

STYLE Attribute

Under HTML and XHTML 1.1, any element can take a style attribute.

Generic Syntax

```
<elem style="...styles...">
```

Notes
The value of this attribute is any combination of style declarations. Because this approach binds the style very tightly to the element in question by placing stylistic information within the document itself, use of the style attribute is discouraged in those cases where a more robust solution (e.g., an embedded or external stylesheet) can be used.

Examples

```
<p style="color: red;">This paragraph's text will be colored red.</p>
<h1 style="font-family: sans-serif; color: magenta; padding: 0.5em;
    border-bottom: 2px solid green; background: cyan;">This H1 will
    assault your visual senses</h1>
```

@import Rule

@import is used to import an external stylesheet in a manner
similar to the LINK element. See the entry for @import in Chapter 3
for details.

Rule Structure

The basis of applying styles to documents is the *rule*. Each rule is
composed of a number of components, each of which has a specific
name and function. These are summarized in Figure 1-1.

The *selector* is the part that determines which portions of the
document will be matched by the rule. The rule's styles will be
applied to the selected element(s). For example, a selector of pre
means that all pre elements will be selected. Multiple selectors
can be grouped in a single rule by separating them with commas.
See Chapter 2 for details about the various selectors which may
be used.

The *declaration block* is bounded by (and includes) a pair of curly
braces. The selector is always to the left of the declaration block
(that is, it comes before the block). Whitespace within a declaration
block is ignored, so any amount of whitespace may be used by
authors to make their styles more readable.

Selector   Declaration Block

```
pre { color: navy; margin: 10px 1em; }
```

Figure 1-1.   CSS rule structure

Inside the declaration block are zero or more *declarations*. Each declaration consists of a *property* followed by a colon, and then the *value* for the property followed by a semicolon. A value will consist of one or more keywords and value types, usually (but not always) separated from each other by a space. The allowed properties and their possible values are discussed in Chapters 4 through 6. There can never be more than one property per declaration.

It is permissible to have an empty declaration block, in which case this rule will apply no styles to the elements matched by the selector. This is functionally equivalent to not writing the rule at all. CSS does not require that the last declaration in a declaration block be followed by a semicolon, but some early CSS1 implementations would incorrectly fail to recognize any styles which followed a declaration block that did not end with a semicolon.

Resolving Style Conflicts

In the course of creating a stylesheet, it is quite possible that many different rules will apply to a single element. For example, if one rule applies to all paragraph elements, and another rule applies to all elements which have a CLASS attribute with a value of urgent, which rule should be used?

As it happens, both rules will apply. If the different rules contain declarations that deal with different properties, then there is no conflict, and the styles are "pooled together." However, if different rules have declarations that attempt to set values for the *same* property, then there are mechanisms to decide which styles will actually be used.

As an example, assume the following three rules:

```
div#aside h1 {color: red; margin: 0.5em;}
h1.title {color: purple; font-weight: bold; margin-left: 3em;}
h1 {color: gray; font-style: italic;}
```

Now assume that the document contains an H1 element which is matched by all three rules. How should it be styled? There are three contradictory values given for color, and there may be some conflict between the margin rules as well.

As it happens, the answer is that our hypothetical H1 should be colored red, boldfaced, italicized, and have top, right, bottom, and left margins of 0.5em. Thus, the declarations which were overruled were color: purple, color: red, and margin-left: 3em. The mechanisms by which we arrived at this answer are further explained in the next section.

Cascade Rules

In determining how to style a document, some declarations may conflict with each other. For example, if two different declarations call for all paragraphs to be either red or blue, which one wins out? This process is described by the *cascade*. The cascade rules are as follows:

1. Find all declarations that apply to the element and property in question, for the target media type (i.e., do not apply print-media styles if the current media is screen). Declarations apply if the associated selector matches the element in question. Thus, the declaration in the rule h6 {color: navy;} will be used only if the document contains one or more H6 elements.

2. The primary sort of the declarations is done by origin and weight. The *origin* refers to the source from which the declaration comes: the author's styles, the user's styles, or the user agent's internal styles (hereafter referred to as the *default stylesheet*). An imported stylesheet has the same origin as the stylesheet that imported it. The *weight* refers to the importance of the declaration. For normal declarations, author stylesheets override user stylesheets which override the default stylesheet. For "!important" declarations, user stylesheets override author stylesheets which override the default stylesheet. "!important" declarations override normal declarations. See "Importance" later in the chapter for more details.

3. The secondary sort is by specificity of selector: more specific selectors will override more general ones. Pseudo-elements and pseudo-classes are counted as normal elements and classes, respectively. See "Specificity Calculation" later in the chapter for more details.

4. Finally, sort by order specified: if two rules have the same weight, origin, and specificity, the latter specified wins. Rules in imported stylesheets are considered to be placed before any rules in the embedded stylesheet.

Specificity Calculation

Every selector in CSS is assigned a *specificity*. The actual specificity is calculated based on the composition of the selector itself, according to the following rules:

1. Count the number of ID selectors in the selector (= a)

2. Count the number of other selectors and pseudo-class selectors in the selector (= b)

3. Count the number of element names in the selector (= c)

4. Ignore pseudo-elements

The concatenation of the three values (a-b-c) yields the specificity. Note that these numbers are *not* represented in base ten; thus 0-0-11 is less than 0-1-0, even though they might be represented as "11" and "10" respectively. It is for this reason that authors are encouraged to think of specificity as a comma- or hyphen-separated list of three numbers. For example:

```
h1 {color: black}                           /* spec. = 0-0-1 */
div ul li {color: gray;}                     /* spec. = 0-0-3 */
pre.example {color: white;}                  /* spec. = 0-1-1 */
div.help h1 em.term {color: blue;}           /* spec. = 0-2-3 */
#title {color: cyan;}                        /* spec. = 1-0-0 */
body ul#first li ol.steps li {color: silver;} /* spec. = 1-1-5 */
```

As detailed earlier in the section "Cascade Rules," specificity is more important than the order in which rules appear. Thus, if the following two selectors match the same element, the declarations from the first will override any conflicting declarations in the second.

```
div.credits {text-align: center; color; gray;}  /* spec. = 0-1-1 */
div {text-align: left; color: black;}            /* spec. = 0-0-1 */
```

Therefore, the element which these two rules match will have gray, centered text.

Important declarations always outweigh non-important declarations, no matter the specificity of their associated selectors (see the next section for more details).

Importance

Declarations may be marked as important using the `!important` construct. This is applied to the actual declarations which are important, not to the selector nor to the rule as a whole. For example:

```
p {color: red; background: yellow !important; font-family: serif;}
```

In this example, only the declaration `background: yellow` is important. The other two declarations are not.

If two or more important declarations involve the same property, then the conflict is resolved using specificity calculations. For example:

```
h2 {color: red !important; font-style: italic;}
h2 {color: green !important;}
```

Since both `color` declarations are important, and both associated selectors have the same specificity, the second rule wins because it comes later in the stylesheet. Thus, `H2` elements will be green and italicized—the font-style declaration is not affected in this case.

Inheritance

Many styles can be inherited from an element to its descendant elements. Any inherited style will be applied to an element unless the property in question is explicitly set through a rule whose selector matches the element. For example, consider these rules:

```
body {color: black;}
p {color: green;}
```

Given this, the color of any paragraph will be green, while the color of all other elements will be black. Note that this overriding of inherited styles takes effect no matter what specificity or importance was attached to the original rule. For example:

```
div#summary {color: black !important;}
p {color: green;}
```

Any paragraphs within a `div` whose `id` attribute has a value of `summary` will still be green, because the explicitly assigned style overrides the inherited style.

However, all properties (except for `page`) can be given a value of `inherit`. This directs the user agent to determine the value of the property for the parent element, and use that value for the current element. Thus, `p {color: inherit;}` will set the color of any paragraph to be the same color as its parent. This has the advantages of upgrading the inheritance mechanism such that a style can be explicitly assigned to inherit, instead of relying on the normal inheritance mechanism as a "fallback."

Shorthand Properties

There are a few properties in CSS which are considered *shorthand properties;* that is, they represent a much larger collection of properties. For example, `margin` is a shorthand for the properties `margin-top`, `margin-right`, `margin-bottom`, and `margin-left`. The following two rules will have exactly the same effect:

```
p {margin: 1em;}
p {margin-top: 1em;
   margin-right: 1em;
   margin-bottom: 1em;
   margin-left: 1em;}
```

Because of this, authors must be sure to avoid conflicts between properties and shorthands, or even between two shorthand properties. For example, consider the following two rules as matching the same element:

```
pre.example {margin: 1em;}
pre {margin-left: 3em;}
```

Due to the operation of the cascade, any `pre` element with a `class` of `example` will have a margin 1em wide, *including the left margin.* The shorthand's effects have masked out the value assigned in the `pre` rule.

Another good example involves `text-decoration`, which is a shorthand for no properties at all but acts much as a shorthand property does. Consider the following rules:

```
h2 {text-decoration: overline;}
h2, h3 {text-decoration: underline;}
```

Given these rules, all H2 elements will be underlined *but not overlined.* The given values of text-decoration do not combine, as each combination of keywords is its own unique value. If it is desirable to decorate H2 elements with both an underline and an overline, then the necessary rule is:

```
h2 {text-decoration: underline overline;}
```

Table 1-1 summarizes the shorthand properties in CSS and what properties they represent.

Shorthand property	Represents
background	background-attachment, background-color, background-image, background-position, background-repeat
border	border-color, border-style, border-width
border-bottom	border-bottom-color, border-bottom-style, border-bottom-width
border-left	border-left-color, border-left-style, border-left-width
border-right	border-right-color, border-right-style, border-right-width
border-top	border-top-color, border-top-style, border-top-width
cue	cue-before, cue-after
font	font-family, font-size, font-style, font-weight, font-variant, line-height (**will also reset** font-size-adjust **and** font-stretch)
list-style	list-style-image, list-style-position, list-style-type
margin	margin-top, margin-right, margin-bottom, margin-left

Table 1-1.   Shorthand Properties

Shorthand property	Represents
outline	outline-color, outline-style, outline-width
padding	padding-top, padding-right, padding-bottom, padding-left
pause	pause-after, pause-before

Table 1-1.   Shorthand Properties *(continued)*

Visual Layout

Although it does contain sections for styling non-visual media, CSS is at its heart a style language for visual presentation. Therefore, since authors will spend so much time worrying about the visual effects of their styles, it is crucial to understand how these effects are constructed and laid out.

There are two basic layout mechanisms in CSS: the box model and the inline layout model. Although they are related, each has its own rules and effects, not all of which are intuitive. In addition, there are special rules to describe how positioned elements are laid out, and how floated elements are placed and sized. These rules are closely modeled on the box model, but there are some important differences.

The Box Model

The fundament of visual display under CSS is the box model. Familiarity with the various components of the box model enables the author to understand how a great many properties interact with each other, and to understand why pages appear as they do (or to figure out what's going wrong in buggy browsers).

Basic Components

A diagram of the basic box model is shown in Figure 1-2.

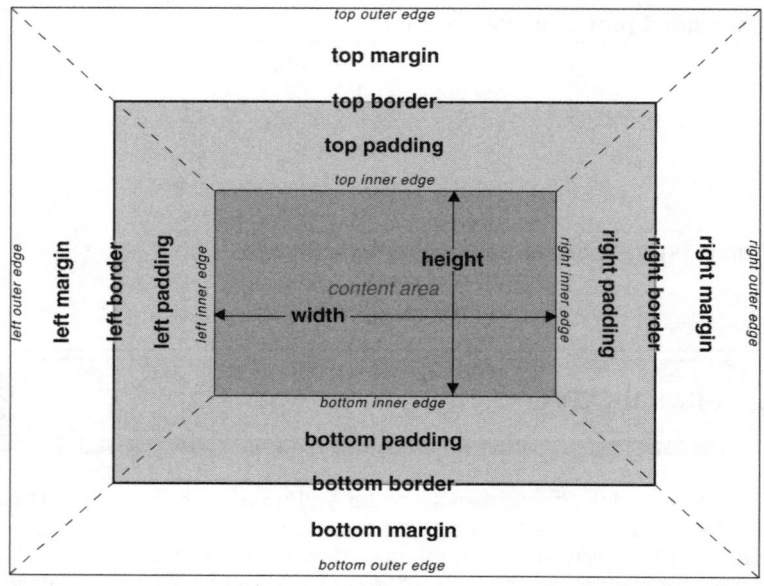

Figure 1-2.   The CSS box model

Specific Layout Rules

The background of an element (whether color, image, or some combination) extends to the outer edge of the border, thus filling the content area and the padding. It will also be visible through any "gaps" in the border itself, such as those seen with the `border-style` values `dotted`, `dashed`, and `double`.

The following equation always holds true: `margin-left + border-left-width + padding-left + width + padding-right + border-right-width + margin-right` = the value of `width` for the parent element (that is, the width of the parent element's content area). This must sometimes be accomplished by setting the left and right margins to negative values. In such cases, the element will appear to be wider than its parent element, and will "stick out" of the content area of its parent. Mathematically, however, the negative margins satisfy the above equation, and so the element can be said to be exactly as wide as the content area of its parent. This may seem disingenuous, since the visual effect is precisely the opposite, but this is permitted under CSS.

Only the margins, `height` and `width` may be set to `auto`. The margins may be given negative lengths, but `height` and `width` may not. The padding and border widths default to `0` (zero), and may not be set to negative lengths.

Vertically adjacent margins of elements in the normal document flow are *collapsed*. In other words, if two margins are vertically adjacent to each other, then the actual distance between the two element borders is the maximum of the adjacent margins. In the case of negative margins, the absolute maximum of the negative adjacent margins is subtracted from the maximum of the positive adjacent margins. The vertically adjacent margins of elements which have been floated or positioned do not collapse.

The mechanism of collapsing margins can be visualized as a paper-and-plastic model. In this model, each element is represented by a piece of paper upon which the element's content has been written (or drawn). Any margins which surround the element are represented as strips of clear plastic attached to the edges of the paper. When one element follows another, they are slid together until the edge of one element's plastic strip touches the edge of the other element's paper. Thus, the plastic will overlap, but the pieces of paper will never be further apart than the width of the wider plastic strip. This holds true even if multiple elements are adjacent, such as one list ending and another beginning. There are four adjacent margins in this example, the bottom margins of the first list and its last list item, and the top margins of the second list and its first list item. The distance between the content of the two list items will be that of the largest of the four margins.

Recall that horizontally adjacent margins do not collapse. Thus, placing 10-pixel margins on two adjacent inline elements will create a 20-pixel space between the right border of the first element and the left border of the second. Margins on floated and positioned elements are never collapsed, either horizontally or vertically.

The Inline Layout Model

Almost as fundamental as the box model is the way in which text is arranged within an element. While this may seem simple, it quickly becomes complex once the details are laid bare.

Basic Components

A diagram of the basic inline layout model is shown in Figure 1-3.

Specific Layout Rules

The height of a line of text is calculated using the following terms:

- **Content area**   The box defined by the `font-size` of each piece of text (whether in an element or not)

- **Half-leading**   The distance determined by the value of `line-height`, where the half-leading equals `((font-size - line-height)/2)`

- **Inline box**   The box defined by subtracting the half-leading from the top and bottom of the content area; for any given piece of text, the height of the inline box will always be equal to the value of `line-height` for that same text

- **Line box**   The actual box which is stacked below the previous line box; this bounds the top of the highest inline box and the bottom of the lowest inline box in the line

How does all this work? For each piece of text, an inline box is generated, using the content area and the half-leading to arrive at its final height. These inline boxes will always be centered vertically within the content area. The inline boxes are then aligned with respect to each other according to the value of `vertical-align` for each. If the value is baseline, then the text baseline is aligned with the baseline of the line.

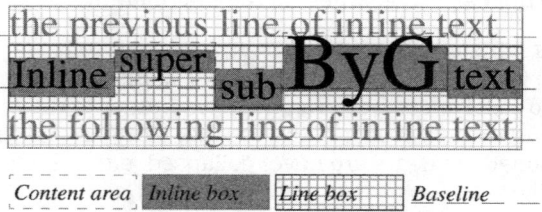

Figure 1-3.   The CSS Inline layout model

Once the inline boxes have been vertically aligned, the height of the line box is determined. The line box's top is aligned with the top of the highest inline box top in the line, and the bottom of the line box is aligned with the bottom of the lowest inline box in the line. The top of each line box is placed adjacent to the bottom of the previous line box, or adjacent to the inner top edge of the parent element in the case of the first line box in the element. Thus the line boxes are "stacked" to form a block-level element's content.

In fact, each character generates its own inline box, but these should all have the same height for a given element, so, in general, inline boxes are discussed at the element level.

Any border which is drawn around an inline element is placed such that it lies just outside the area defined by the content area plus any declared padding. This has no direct relation to the line box itself; the border may be drawn in the same place as the edges of the line box, but if so it is by coincidence. It is entirely possible for an inline element's border to "cut through" the text in the line, or through other lines of text.

When it comes to borders, background, and other box properties, inline elements are formatted as if they were a single line of text. Let's start with the simplest analogy. Picture a given inline element: a single strip of paper with the element's content written upon it. Any backgrounds, borders, padding, and so forth are applied to the inline element as per the box model. The strip of paper is then torn into pieces between words such that each paper segment will fit between the right and left edges of the block-level element's content area. Therefore, borders will most likely not "cap off" the ends of any line segments, except the left edge of the first line segment and the right edge of the last line segment. Similarly, any right or left padding (or margin) will appear only on the last or first line segment, respectively.

This analogy is only partly accurate. If all of the text in the inline element is the same size and has the same vertical alignment, then the analogy is exactly correct. However, if this is not the case, then each line's height will be altered as described earlier in this section. In other words, some line segments could be taller than others in the same inline element, due to the way line boxes are constructed. Otherwise, the analogy holds; any left or right padding or margins will still be applied only to the first or last line segments, respectively.

Setting top and bottom margins on non-replaced inline elements (e.g., elements which contain only text) will have no effect on layout, as margins cannot affect the calculation of the height of a line box. Setting a top and bottom padding may cause the background of the inline element to be increased, but the specification is not clear about what should happen in such a case. It may be that the expanded background will overwrite content in other lines of text, or even in other elements. It is also possible that the backgrounds will be drawn "beneath" the content of other inline elements. User agents are permitted to ignore top and bottom padding on inline elements.

Inline replaced elements (e.g., images within a line of text) are treated a little differently from text. The inline box of a replaced element is defined to be the element *plus* any borders and margins. Thus, top and bottom margins on inline replaced elements can affect the height of a line box.

Float Rules

When an element is floated, its visual placement is governed by a set of ten rules. In effect, these rules say "place the floated element as high, and as far to one side, as possible." However, the details are important:

1. The left outer edge of a left-floating box may not be to the left of the left edge of its containing block. An analogous rule holds for right-floating elements.

2. If the current box is left-floating, and there are any left floating boxes generated by elements earlier in the source document, then for each such earlier box, either the left outer edge of the current box must be to the right of the right outer edge of the earlier box, or its top must be lower than the bottom of the earlier box. Analogous rules hold for right-floating boxes.

3. The right outer edge of a left-floating box may not be to the right of the left outer edge of any right-floating box that is to the right of it. Analogous rules hold for right-floating elements.

4. A floating box's outer top may not be higher than the top of its containing block.

5. The outer top of a floating box may not be higher than the outer top of any block or floated box generated by an element earlier in the source document.

6. The outer top of an element's floating box may not be higher than the top of any line-box containing a box generated by an element earlier in the source document.

7. A left-floating box that has another left-floating box to its left may not have its right outer edge to the right of its containing block's right edge. (Loosely: a left float may not stick out at the right edge, unless it is already as far to the left as possible.) An analogous rule holds for right-floating elements.

8. A floating box must be placed as high as possible.

9. A left-floating box must be put as far to the left as possible, a right-floating box as far to the right as possible. A higher position is preferred over one that is further to the left/right.

10. The top outer edge of the float must be below the bottom outer edge of all earlier left-floating boxes (in the case of `clear: left`), or all earlier right-floating boxes (in the case of `clear: right`), or both (`clear: both`).

The margins of floated elements are never collapsed. Thus, even though an element may be floated into the top left corner of its parent element, its margins will push it away from the corner, and will push any content away from the floated element.

Even though floated elements are prohibited from being any higher than the top of the containing block, there is a way around this. By setting a negative top margin, the element can be "pulled up" past the top of its containing block. This is somewhat similar to the ability of elements to be wider than their containing block through the use of negative left and right margins. As well, floating elements can be pulled out of an element by setting a negative left or right margin. However, the user agent is *not* required to reflow the document to account for this situation, so a floating element with negative margins may overlap other content within the document. Authors are advised to use this technique very cautiously.

Although floating elements are removed from the normal flow of the document, they do affect the layout of content within the document. This is effectively done by increasing the padding within any following elements on those lines which are next to a floating element. However, this means that the backgrounds and borders of any elements will extend "underneath" the floated element, and possibly past the other side of the floated element. This behavior ensures that all element boxes will remain rectangular, but it can lead to unwanted effects.

Positioning Rules

Although CSS started out as a way to style elements in the normal flow of a document, it quickly became apparent that authors wanted to do more with their layouts. There were requests for a CSS way to replace frames, methods to offset elements from their normal placement, and more. In response, positioning was added to the specification in CSS2. There are really only three kinds of positioning: static, relative, and absolute. Static positioning is the state of normality—in other words, an "un-positioned" paragraph actually has a static position. Relatively positioned elements are offset from their normal place in the document, while absolutely positioned elements are placed with respect to some point, and they never move from that position.

Every positioned element is placed with respect to its *containing block*. This block can be thought of as the positioning context for the positioned element. Every positioned element has its own unique containing block. The way to determine such a block is explained in each following section.

Relative Positioning

Relative positioning is fairly simple in its execution. A relatively positioned element is offset from the place it would ordinarily occupy in the normal document flow, and the space it leaves behind is preserved. This makes it fairly likely that the positioned element will overlap other elements and their content, or be overlapped by other elements, depending on the value of the property z-index. It is up to the author to construct styles that avoid such situations, if desired.

Containing Block
The containing block of a relatively positioned element is the box it would have occupied in the normal flow of the document (i.e., had it not been positioned).

Offsets
The distance of a relatively positioned element is set with the properties top, right, bottom, and left. Positive values will push the element toward the center of its containing block, and negative values will push it away. Thus, a positive value for top will push

the element downward, while a positive value for `bottom` will move it upward. Negative values will reverse the directions. Similarly, a positive value for `left` will push the element to the right, and a positive `right` value will move it to the left, with negative values having the opposite effects.There are cases where the values of some properties will clash with each other. For example, setting both `top` and `bottom` to `10px` means that the element should be moved both upward and downward by 10 pixels, which is not possible. Therefore, the following rules are used:

1. If the properties `top` and `bottom` are both given an explicit value, then the value of `bottom` is ignored.

2. If the properties `left` and `right` are both given an explicit value, then the value of `right` is ignored in left-to-right languages. In right-to-left languages, `left` is ignored.

Absolute Positioning

Absolute positioning actually covers two values of the property `position`. These values are `absolute` and `fixed`. The only real difference between the two is the containing block used in each case; otherwise, the rules explained in this section are the same for both.

In both cases, the positioned element is entirely removed from the normal flow of the document. This makes it quite likely that the positioned element will overlap other elements and their content, or be overlapped by other elements, depending on the value of the property `z-index`. It is up to the author to construct styles that avoid such situations, if desired.

Containing Block

In the case of `position: absolute`, the containing block of the positioned element is the nearest ancestor element which has a value for the property `position` other than `static`. If no such ancestor exists, then the containing block is the root element of the document. In HTML and XHTML, this is effectively the `HTML` element, and *not* the `BODY` element. This will start the containing block at the top left corner of the document, *outside* any margins set on the `BODY` element. Absolutely positioned elements still scroll with the rest of the document, as they have been absolutely positioned with respect to the document itself.

In the case of `position: fixed`, the containing block is the *viewport*. In Web browsers, the viewport is the browser's display window, which means that fixed-position elements will not scroll with the document and can thus be used in a manner similar to frames. In paged media such as a printout, each page establishes its own viewport, so a fixed-position element will appear in the same place on each page.

Horizontal Dimensions

The horizontal dimensions of an absolutely positioned element are set with the properties `left`, `margin-left`, `border-left-width`, `padding-left`, `width`, `padding-right`, `border-right-width`, `margin-right`, and `right`. The values of these properties, when added together, *must* equal the width of the containing block. Negative margins may make the element wider than its containing block.

There are a number of rules which govern the adjustment of these property values. The rules for non-replaced elements (e.g., paragraphs) are as follows:

1. If the property `left` is set to `auto` in left-to-right languages, then the value is reset to be aligned with the same place where the element's left edge would have been if it still were a part of the normal flow of the document (i.e., it had not been positioned). If that point is to the left of the left edge of the containing block, then `left` will be set to a negative value. In right-to-left languages, this rule is applied to the property `right`, not `left`.

2. If the property `width` is set to `auto`, then any auto values for the properties `left` and `right` are reset to 0. This will have the effect of marking the element and its margins as wide as the containing block.

3. If the properties `left`, `right`, or `width` are set to `auto`, then any `auto` values for the properties `margin-left` and `margin-right` are reset to 0. This will remove any left or right margins from the element.

4. If the properties `margin-left` and `margin-right` are both set to `auto`, then they are set to be of equal widths. If the element's width is set to an explicit length, then this will have the effect of "centering" the element within its containing block. (If the element's `width` is not set to an explicit length,

then it must be `auto` and the above rule will take effect, setting both margins to `0`.)

5. If there is only one property whose value remains `auto` (i.e., it is not reset by one of the previous rules), then it is reset to be the length necessary to satisfy the equation for calculating horizontal dimensions.

6. If all dimensions are set to explicit lengths, and these lengths do not add up to the width of the containing block, then in left-to-right languages the value of the property `left` is reset such that the equation for calculating horizontal dimensions will be satisfied. In right-to-left languages, it is the property `right` which is reset.

For replaced elements (e.g., images) which have been absolutely positioned, the rules differ from the ones just described in two ways. First, if the property `width` has a value of `auto`, replace it with the intrinsic width of the element. Second, since the value of the property `width` can never be `auto`, the third rule (listed previously) is effectively ignored.

In addition, the width of an element can be bounded by the properties `min-width` and `max-width`. These are handled using the following rules:

1. The width is computed as normal (see previous rules).

2. If the value given for the property `min-width` is greater than that given for `max-width`, the value of `max-width` is reset to the value of `min-width`.

3. If the computed width of the element is greater than `max-width`, or smaller than `min-width`, then the value of the property `width` is reset to match the appropriate bounding property.

It may be that a user agent defines its own value for `min-width`. If so, then the user agent is free to reset any value for `min-width` which falls below its internal value.

Vertical Dimensions

The vertical dimensions of an absolutely positioned element are set with the properties `top`, `margin-top`, `border-top-width`, `padding-top`, `height`, `padding-bottom`, `border-bottom-width`, `margin-bottom`, and `bottom`. The values of these properties, when added together, *must* equal the height of the containing block. Negative margins may make the element taller than its containing block.

There are a number of rules which govern the adjustment of these property values. The rules for non-replaced elements (e.g., paragraphs) are set out in CSS2 as follows:

1. If the property `top` is set to `auto`, then the value is reset to be aligned with the same place where the element's top edge would have been if it still were a part of the normal flow of the document (i.e., it had not been positioned). If that point is above the containing block, then `top` will be set to a negative value.

2. If the properties `height` and `bottom` are both set to `auto`, then `bottom` is reset to `0`.

3. If either of the properties `bottom` or `height` are set to `auto`, then any `auto` values for the properties `margin-top` and `margin-bottom` are reset to `0`. This will remove any top or bottom margins from the element.

4. If the properties `margin-top` and `margin-bottom` are both set to `auto`, then they are set to be of equal heights. If the element's height is set to an explicit length, then this will have the effect of "vertically centering" the element within its containing block. (If the element's `height` is not set to an explicit length, this means it is set to `auto` and the previous rule will take effect, setting both margins to `0`.)

5. If there is only one property whose value remains `auto` (i.e., it is not reset by one of the previous rules), then it is reset to be the length necessary to satisfy the equation for calculating horizontal dimensions.

6. If all dimensions are set to explicit lengths, and these lengths do not add up to the height of the containing block, then the value of the property `bottom` is reset such that the equation for calculating horizontal dimensions will be satisfied.

For replaced elements (e.g., images) which have been absolutely positioned, the rules differ from the ones just described in two ways. First, if the property `height` has a value of `auto`, replace it with the intrinsic height of the element. Second, since the value of the property `height` can never be `auto`, the third rule (listed previously) is effectively ignored.

In addition, the height of an element can be bounded by the properties `min-height` and `max-height`. These are handled using the following rules:

1. The height is computed as normal (see previous rules).

2. If the value given for the property `min-height` is greater than that given for `max-height`, the value of `max-height` is reset to the value of `min-height`.

3. If the computed height of the element is greater than `max-height`, or smaller than `min-height`, then the value of the property `height` is reset to match the appropriate bounding property.

It may be that a user agent defines its own value for `min-height`. If so, then the user agent is free to reset any value for `min-height` which falls below its internal value.

Note that under these rules, it is impossible to set a combination of property values which will cause an element to be just tall enough to contain its own content, and no taller (or shorter). This effect is sometimes called "shrink wrapping," and its omission has been seen as a serious shortcoming in CSS2. To redress this situation, there have been proposed errata which change the meaning of `height: auto` to "make the element tall enough to display its own content." These errata have not been formally adopted by the W3C, but they are supported by every known user agent which supports absolute positioning.

As a basic example, assume for an absolutely positioned element that both margins and padding are set to 10 pixels in width, the borders have zero width, and the `height` of the positioned element is `auto`. Further assume that `top` is set to `0`, and `bottom` is set to `100px`. Now, further assume that the content is 260 pixels tall once it has been rendered. This will effectively set `height` to `260px`. This means that the positioning context would have to be exactly 400 pixels tall in order to satisfy the equation for calculating vertical dimensions. If the positioning context is actually 475 pixels tall, then `bottom` will be reset to `175px`.

Font Rules

When a user agent renders text, it must select a font to use. However, almost no font in existence contains every possible character which might be needed in a document. Thus, the truth is that text is rendered a character at a time, with the user agent doing its best to locate the needed character from its list of available fonts. It must not only determine that a character exists, but also whether or not it is available in the style, weight, and variant which may be requested by the document's CSS rules.

In these rules, a *font family* is actually a collection of font faces given a common name. For example, Times New Roman is really a collection of font faces. Each face depicts a variant of the basic font; thus, the collection may contain Times New Roman Italic, Times New Roman Bold, and so on. Therefore, a *font face* is a variant on the default font in the font family. Thus, the default font will have a name something like Times New Roman Regular.

Authors do not actually select these faces by name, but instead express preferences for the kind of face they would like to use through various font-related properties. See the property `font`, and its related properties, in Chapter 4 for more details.

Font Family Matching

The author (or the user) can influence this selection process by providing a list of fonts to be used, in order of preference, in the rendering of an element. The user agent utilizes this list as a part of the rules for picking which font family to use for the rendering of a given character.

The steps involved in font matching are as follows:

1. In the rendering of a character of text, the user agent builds a list of font properties which are applicable to the character. The user agent then identifies a font family which would appear to contain those characteristics, as well as the needed character.

2. If the needed font face cannot be found within the family, the user agent can attempt advanced handling (described later).

3. If steps 1 and 2 fail, then the user agent should proceed to the next font family in its font list. The process of font face matching is described in the next section.

4. If the needed font face can be found within the font family, but the needed character does not exist, then the user agent should proceed to the next font family in its font list.

5. If the needed character cannot be found in the needed font face, then the user agent should indicate that the proper character cannot be displayed (e.g., fill the space with a "missing character" open square).

For example, assume an author declares that an H2 element should be rendered using Helvetica, and that the text within that element should be boldfaced and italicized. The user agent must first locate the font family Helvetica and then determine if it contains a font face which is both boldfaced and italicized. If such a face exists, then the user agent checks to make sure that the needed character exists within the face. If it does, then it is used to render the character, and the user agent moves on to the next character to start the process over. If the character does not exist in the font face, then the user agent must look to other fonts to see if they have the needed character in an appropriate face. If the user agent cannot come up with a suitable match, then it must use a "missing character" symbol to indicate its failure.

CSS2 provides rules (as mentioned in item 2 in the previous list) for more advanced handling of font matching. These are:

1. **Intelligent font matching.** The user agent uses font descriptors such as glyph widths and x-height to identify an alternate font family choice. If it determines that a match exists, then that font is used to render the character. This does not change the value of the property `font-family`.

2. **Font downloading.** The user agent attempts to identify a font resource which it can download and use. It is up to the user agent to decide whether a given font resource will be useful, and if so, what to do while it waits for the font to finish downloading.

3. **Font synthesis.** The user agent can attempt to construct its own font, based on font descriptors such as the panose-1 and x-height values. In fact, all font descriptors must be provided for font synthesis to take place.

User agents are not required to support any of these advanced mechanisms.

Font Face Matching

During the font family matching process, the user agent must determine if a font has the necessary font face available. For example, if the author has specified that an element should be italicized, the user agent must find an italic face of the font being used. Faces are matched as follows:

1. The user agent first attempts to match the face declared in font-style. If the value given is italic, then any face labeled *Italic* or *Oblique* will match. If the value given is oblique, then only *Oblique* faces will match.

2. The user agent next attempts to match the face declared in font-variant. If the value given is small-caps, then any face labeled *Small-caps* will match. If no such face exists, then the user agent can generate a substitute by scaling capital letters from a regular face as needed. As a last resort, the user agent can use regular capital letters with no scaling. If the value given is normal, then any face not labeled *Small-caps* will match.

3. The user agent matches the value of font-weight. Font weight matching is described in the next section, and the match can never fail.

4. Last, the font's size is matched. Since most fonts can be scaled to any necessary size, this step should never fail.

For example, assume that an author has directed that an element should be both small-caps and italic. The user agent must locate a face which is both small-caps and italic, if possible. Otherwise, it keeps looking for a match using the rules given in the previous section.

Font Weight Matching

The property font-weight can accept a number of values, including the nine numeric values 100 through 900 and the values normal and bold. The numeric values are the core of font-weight matching; the other values (e.g., bold) are treated as human-friendly labels for defined points on the numeric scale. The weight of a font is matched as follows:

- The value `normal` corresponds to the value `400`; `bold` corresponds to `700`.

- If the font already has a nine-level weight scale, as in font formats such as OpenType, that scale is mapped to the values `100` through `900`.

- If a font has a face labeled *Medium* as well as one of the labels *Book*, *Regular*, *Roman*, or *Normal*, then *Medium* corresponds to the value `500`.

- If the font has a face labeled *Bold*, that face corresponds to the value `700`.

If the font contains fewer than nine weights, then the "gaps" are filled as follows:

- If the value `500` is unassigned, it corresponds to the same face as that used for the value `400`.

- If any of the values `600`, `700`, `800`, or `900` are unassigned, then they correspond to the next darker weight available. If no darker weight is available, then they correspond to the next lighter weight.

- If any of the values `100`, `200`, or `300` are unassigned, then they correspond to the next lighter weight available. If no lighter weight is available, then correspond to the next darker weight.

The majority of fonts will have at least two faces: normal and bold, which are mapped to the values `400` and `700`. In such a case, the values `100` through `500` will result in a normal face, while `600` through `900` will yield the darker face.

Let's pick a more complicated example. Assume a font which contains the following four faces: Meyer Regular, Meyer Bold, Meyer Light, and Meyer Dark. This last is even darker than the "bold" face. Given these faces, the weight numbers will be assigned as follows:

- Meyer Light: `100`, `200`, `300`
- Meyer Regular: `400`, `500`

- Meyer Bold: 600, 700
- Meyer Dark: 800, 900

If Meyer Light had not been available as part of the font family, then Meyer Regular would have been the face used for the values 100 through 500. The rest of the assignments would have gone unchanged.

Chapter 2
Values

Although authors tend to focus on the properties in CSS, nothing in CSS would work without the values that are assigned to those properties. After all, you can't describe the left border of an element without being able to say what it looks like, and that's what values do. In many cases, a property will use its own uniquely defined keywords (e.g., underline or thin). However, there are also many cases where generic types of values can be used. These generic value types are explained in this chapter.

Value Representations

The property reference chapters (4 through 6) use roughly the same value syntax as that described in section 1.3.2 of the CSS2 specification. In particular, the same symbolic conventions are used to indicate alternatives and optional keywords. The *grouping symbols* are as follows:

- A vertical bar (|) is used to separate two or more alternatives when any one, but only one, of them may be used.

- A double vertical bar (| |) is used to separate two or more alternatives when any of them may be used in any order. This operator is stronger than the single vertical bar.

- A sequence of several words means that all of them must occur in the order shown. 2A sequence is stronger than the double vertical bar.

- Square brackets ([ ]) are used to group values together.

Thus, the following two expressions are equivalent:

```
x y || a b | c || m | n
[x y] || [[a b] | c] || [m | n]
```

In addition to the grouping symbols, there are also *modifier symbols*. Any keyword, value type, or group can be modified using the following symbols.

- An asterisk (*) indicates that the preceding value or group may occur zero or more times, with no defined upper limit.

- A plus sign (+) indicates that the preceding value or group must occur one or more times, with no defined upper limit.

- A question mark (?) indicates that the preceding value or group is optional.

- A pair of two comma-separated numbers in curly braces ({X,Y}) indicates that the preceding value or group occurs a minimum of X times and a maximum of Y times. For example, test{2,5} means that the word test must appear anywhere from two to five times.

Any symbols besides the ones defined here must appear literally. Two such examples are the comma (,) and slash (/) symbols.

Basic Rules

The most important thing to keep in mind with values is that, when they use a unit, there is no space between the value and its unit. For example, a distance of four inches is written 4in. Any space between the value and its associated unit (as in 4 in) will cause browsers to ignore the declaration at best, and drastically misinterpret it at worst. This is one of the most common mistakes CSS authors make.

It is also the case that values are *never* quoted (except for string values and some font names). Thus, the keyword value for the color blue should *not* be written "blue". Instead, it should be blue. This is possibly the second most common mistake committed by CSS authors.

Value Reference

Color Values

Color values are used to specify a color (go figure). Typically, these are used to set a color either for the foreground of an element (i.e., its text) or else for the background of the element. They can also be used to affect the color of borders and other decorative effects. Any color value is referred to in the property reference chapters as <color>.

Value Types

#RRGGBB
#RRGGBB is the familiar color value format used by traditional HTML authors. In this format, the first pair of digits corresponds to the red setting, the second pair to green, and the third pair to blue. Each pair is in hexadecimal notation in the range 00 - FF. Thus, a "pure" green is represented as #00FF00, "pure" red is written #FF0000, medium gray is #808080, and so forth.

#RGB
This is a shorter form of the six-digit notation just described. In this format, each digit is replicated to arrive at an equivalent six-digit value; thus, #6A7 becomes #66AA77, "pure" green is represented as #0F0, and so forth. Medium gray cannot be exactly represented in this format, since it does not use replicated pairs, but it can be approximated as either #777 or #888.

rgb(rrr%,ggg%,bbb%)
This format allows the author to declare RGB values in the range 0% to 100%. Decimal values are permitted (e.g., 57.5%). Any values outside the allowed range are clipped to the closest edge of the range, so that −50% would be clipped to 0%. The value for black is represented as rgb(0%,0%,0%), "pure" green is written rgb(0%,100%,0%), medium gray is rgb(50%,50%,50%), and so forth.

rgb(rrr,ggg,bbb)
The difference between this format and the previous one is that the accepted range of values is 0 - 255. Not coincidentally, this range is the decimal equivalent of 00 - FF in hexadecimal notation. As with the percentage RGB values, any numbers outside the allowed range are clipped to the edges of the range, so 300 would be clipped to 255. In this format, "pure" blue is represented as rgb(0,0,255), white is written rgb(255,255,255), medium gray is rgb(128,128,128), and so forth.

<keyword>
CSS defines 16 keywords, which are based on the original Windows VGA palette. The defined keywords are aqua, black, blue, fuchsia, gray, green, lime, maroon, navy, olive, purple, red, silver, teal, white, and yellow. Some browsers may

recognize other keywords, but these are not (as of this writing) found in any specification and are not guaranteed to work consistently between browsers, or indeed from version to version in a single browser.

Notes

Any color value which goes outside the color range of the display medium will be clipped to the nearest "edge" of the supported colorspace. All RGB colors in CSS are specified in relation to the sRGB specification; see `http://www.w3.org/Graphics/Color/sRGB.html` for more details.

Color choices should be made with legibility and visual impairments in mind. For example, various forms of color blindness make it difficult to distinguish between red and green, or red and blue; see the Web Accessibility Initiative (WAI) area of `http://www.w3.org/` for more information.

Allowed Properties

The properties which can accept color values are

```
border-color              border-right
border-top-color          border-bottom
border-right-color        border-left
border-bottom-color       color
border-left-color         background-color
border                    text-shadow
border-top                outline-color
```

Length Values

Absolute-length values are those which describe a length in the real world, whereas relative-length values describe a length in relation to some other measure. They are formatted as an optional sign (plus or minus) followed by a number, followed by a length unit identifier. Any length value is referred to in the property reference chapters as `<length>`.

Value Types

in (inches)

These are the very inches one can find on almost any American ruler. Although these might seem to be well-defined, the translation from real world measures to display environments is often ill-defined. For example, in order to accurately make a font one inch tall, the computer must know precisely the dimensions of its display environment, and how many pixels there are per inch. This can vary widely between a 17" monitor and, say, a projection display in a lecture hall. Typically, the only environment in which length measures can be precisely defined is in print media.

cm (centimeters)

This is the basis of measurement in the non-American part of the world, and a unit generally found even on American rulers. There are 2.54 centimeters to an inch, and one centimeter equals 0.394 inches. As with inches, the translation of centimeters to a display environment is ill-defined and likely to be inaccurate.

mm (millimeters)

As almost the entire world knows, there are 10 millimeters to a centimeter (so you get 25.4 millimeters to an inch, whereas 1 millimeter equals 0.0394 inches). The same translation-to-display warning applies to millimeters as well as centimeters and inches.

pt (points)

These are traditional typographical units, and are familiar to most modern authors because they are used to define text size in every popular word-processing program available in the Western world. By definition, there are 72 points to an inch, since points were defined in a pre-metric era. Therefore, the capital letters of text set to 12 points should be a sixth of an inch tall. Points are widely used on the Web, but as with the other absolute-length units, they do not map consistently into display environments. For example, `12pt` = 12 pixels on most Macintosh systems, whereas Windows systems may map `12pt` to 16 pixels, or 22 pixels, or any number of other pixels. For this reason, points are strongly discouraged as a unit of measure in screen media. In print media, points are far less dangerous and can even be quite useful.

2

pc (picas)

A pica is equivalent to 12 points, so there are 6 picas to an inch. As described in the previous listing, the capital letters of text set to 1 pica should be a sixth of an inch tall. Also, the same warnings about translating to display environments apply here.

em (em-height)

In CSS, `1em` is equivalent to the height of the character box for a given font. Ems can be used to set relative sizes for fonts; for example, `1.2em` is the same as saying `120%`.

ex (x-height)

This refers to the x-height of the font, which is generally defined to be the height of a lowercase "`x`" that exists in the chosen font. Unfortunately, the overwhelming majority of fonts available today do not include a defined x-height, so most browsers approximate `1ex` as `0.5em`. The exception to this crude approximation is Internet Explorer 5 for Macintosh, which attempts to determine the actual x-height of a font by internally bitmapping an "x" and counting the pixels.

px (pixels)

Every computer display is composed of pixels, which are the small dots that make up the entire image. In CSS terms, however, a pixel is defined to be about the size required to yield 90 pixels per inch. Most user agents ignore this in favor of simply addressing the pixels on the monitor. Scaling factors may be used when printing, in order to compensate for the high pixel density of modern printers.

Notes

If a negative length value is allowed on a given property but cannot be supported by the user agent, the value should be converted to the closest supported value. This will most likely mean 0, but it could be some other value.

A length value of 0 does not need one of the unit identifiers to follow it. Any other length value (positive or negative) *must* have a unit identifier, or it will be ignored by correctly written user agents.

Allowed Properties

The properties which can accept length values are

margin	right
margin-top	top
margin-right	width
margin-bottom	max-width
margin-left	min-width
padding	height
padding-bottom	max-height
padding-right	min-height
padding-left	line-height
padding-top	vertical-align
border-top-width	marker-offset
border-width	size
border-right-width	background-position
border-bottom-width	font-size
border-left-width	text-indent
border	text-shadow
border-top	letter-spacing
border-right	word-spacing
border-bottom	border-spacing
border-left	outline
bottom	outline-width
left	

Angle Values

Angle values are formatted as an optional sign (plus or minus) followed by a number, followed by an angle unit identifier. Any angle value is referred to in the property reference chapters as <angle>.

Value Types

deg (degrees)
Degrees describe angles using the range 0 – 360, as on compasses; thus a right angle would be 90deg.

grad (gradians)
Gradians describe angles using the range 0–400; thus a right angle would be 100grad.

rad (radians)
Radians describe angles using the range 0–pi (3.14159...); thus a
right angle would be `1.57079rad`.

Notes

Negative angles are permitted, but will be converted to their positive
equivalent. Thus, a value of `−90deg` will be converted to `270deg`.

Under CSS2, angle values are used only in aural styles. Because no
support for aural styles was present at the time of writing, there
was no known support for angle values.

Allowed Properties

The properties which can accept angle values are

```
azimuth
elevation
```

Time Values

Time values are formatted as a number followed by a time unit
identifier; thus time values cannot be negative. Any time value is
referred to in the property reference chapters as `<time>`.

Value Types

s (seconds)
Time measures of a full second.

ms (milliseconds)
Time measures of one-thousandth of a second; thus `1000ms`
equals `1s`.

Notes

Under CSS2, time values are used only in aural styles. Because no
support for aural styles was present at the time of writing, there
was no known support for time values.

Allowed Properties

The properties which can accept time values are

```
pause
pause-after
pause-before
```

Frequency Values

Frequency values are formatted as a number followed by a frequency unit identifier; thus frequency values cannot be negative. Any frequency value is referred to in the property reference chapters as <frequency>.

Value Types

hz (Hertz)
The frequency is defined using the Hertz scale.

khz (kilohertz)
The frequency is defined using the kilohertz scale.

Notes
Under CSS2, frequency values are used only in aural styles. Because no support for aural styles was present at the time of writing, there was no known support for time values.

Allowed Properties
The properties which can accept frequency values are

pitch

Strings

String values are used in very rare circumstances, but can be quite powerful when employed. Any string value is referred to in the property reference chapters as <string>.

Value Types

<string>
Any arbitrary sequence of characters can be codified as a string. The sequence is enclosed in quotation marks, either single or double. If a string is broken across multiple lines for any reason, each newline must be preceded by a backslash. Newline characters cannot directly occur inside a string, but they can be represented using the sequence \A ("A" being the hexadecimal code for a newline in Unicode).

Notes

If quotation marks need to appear within a string value, then the author should be sure that they are not the same type as those which enclose the value. If they are the same, then the quotation marks inside the string must be escaped using a backslash character (\). For example:

```
content: "The man said, \"Help me!\" so I did.";
```

The same would have to be done for single-quote marks inside a string value enclosed by single-quote marks.

Allowed Properties

The properties which can accept string values are

```
content
quotes
text-align
```

Percentages

Percentage values are formatted as an optional sign (plus or minus) followed by a number (either real or integer) followed by a percent sign (%). Any percentage value is referred to in the property reference chapters as <percentage>.

Value Types

<percentage>

Percentage values are always used to express a value in relation to another one, such as setting a font to be half again as big as its parent element's font with the value 150%. Percentages are calculated in relation to different things for different properties; see the property references for information on each property which accepts percentages.

Notes

The resulting value for a percentage calculation is inherited to descendant elements; thus, if a font's size is calculated to be 19 pixels tall, then that size is inherited, not the percentage.

Allowed Properties

The properties which can accept percentage values are

bottom

left

right

top

width

max-width

min-width

height

max-height

min-height

line-height

vertical-align

background-position

font-size

text-indent

volume

pause

pause-after

pause-before

URI Values

URI values are used to point to files or other resources external to the stylesheet. Any URL value is referred to in the property reference chapters as <uri>.

Value Types

url(<uri>)

This construct is used to refer to files external to both the stylesheet and the base document. The only type of file which browsers will generally recognize are graphic files, although in principle any kind of file could be pointed to using this value type.

Notes

Under CSS, relative URI values are always in relation to the stylesheet itself. If the stylesheet is embedded in the document, then the URI will by coincidence be in relation to the document, but only because the document and the stylesheet are in the same location. Unfortunately, Navigator 4.x interprets URIs in relation to the document itself, not the stylesheet. Therefore, it is sometimes advised that authors only use absolute URIs in their stylesheets.

Allowed Properties

The properties which can accept URI values are

content

list-style-image

background-image

cursor

cue-after

cue-before

play-during

Chapter 3
Selectors, Pseudo-Classes, Pseudo-Elements, and At-Rules

Although the long list of allowed properties and values is very important to CSS, it is even more important to know how and where those properties can be applied to documents. This is accomplished with selectors, pseudo-classes, pseudo-elements, and a collection of what are called at-rules.

Selectors

In order to associate styles with a specific element or set of elements, it is necessary to create a selector. This is the part of a style rule which selects an element or set of elements and therefore causes the styles to be applied to them. There are many kinds of selectors.

Type Selector

A *type selector* is one which selects elements in the document's language type. (In CSS1, this was called an *element selector*.) These are the simplest kinds of selectors.

Generic Syntax

x
Matches any element X.

Notes

Under HTML and XHTML, these will be the familiar document elements like H2, PRE, TABLE, and so on. In other markup languages, the permitted type selectors will be the range of elements permitted in that particular markup language.

Examples

```
h3 {color: maroon;}
p {font-family: serif; text-decoration: overline;}
```

Descendant Selector

A *descendant selector* is used to select elements which are descendants of another element in the document tree. (In CSS1, this was called a *contextual selector*.)

Generic Syntax

`X Y Z`

Matches any element Z which is a descendant of element Y, which is in turn a descendant of element X.

Notes

A descendant selector is composed of a space-separated list of two or more selectors. Note that the descendant can be of any relation, from a direct child to a great-great-great-great-grandchild, or even further. Thus, the selector `div strong` will select a STRONG element which is contained within a DIV element, no matter how many "levels deep" the STRONG may be found. To select an element which is the child of another, see the child selector section later in this chapter.

There have been reports of cases where complicated descendant selectors have confused Navigator 4.x. These cases seem to be fairly rare, and are difficult to reproduce when they do occur.

Examples

```
h1 em {font-style: italic;}
div p {background: lime;}
```

Universal Selector

The *universal selector* is used to select any element.

Generic Syntax

`*`

Matches any element.

Notes

The universal selector is treated much like a wild-card symbol in regular expressions. It can be used to ensure that elements of a sufficiently removed relation to the parent element are selected; for example, `div * p` will only select paragraphs that are no closer than grandchildren of a DIV. Any paragraph which is a child of the DIV will *not* be selected.

If no selector is present in a rule, then the universal selector is implied.

Examples

```
*  {color: black;}
div * p {border: 1px solid green;}
```

Child Selector

A *child selector* is used to select an element which is a direct child of another element.

Generic Syntax

```
X > Y
```

Selects any element Y which is a child of element X. Any deeper relationship (such as a grandchild element) will not be selected.

Notes

Due to its nature, a child selector must have at least two regular selectors separated by the > symbol. The whitespace around the > symbol is entirely optional.

Internet Explorer 4 has problems handling this selector, and often will match the last type selector in the expression, regardless of its context. In other words, em > strong will incorrectly match all STRONG elements in the document.

Examples

```
div  > p {margin-top: 1.5em;}
li>ul {list-style-type: square;}
td > a:link {color: white; background: black;}
```

Adjacent-Sibling Selector

An *adjacent-sibling selector* will select an element which immediately follows another element in the document markup.

Generic Syntax

`X + Y`

Selects any element Y which immediately follows element X.

Notes

Due to its nature, an adjacent-sibling selector must have at least two regular selectors separated by the + symbol. The whitespace around the + symbol is entirely optional.

Any text which appears between two elements will not affect the operation of this selector, unless that text is contained within an element which is sibling to the other two elements. Thus, if a paragraph is followed by some text which is followed by a DIV, then the text between the two does not affect sibling adjacency. If the intervening text were enclosed in an H3 element, then the H3 would prevent the paragraph and the DIV from being adjacent siblings. Similarly, if two inline elements are separated by text, they are still adjacent siblings.

Internet Explorer 4 and 5 both have problems handling this selector, and often will match the last type selector in the expression, regardless of its context. In other words, em + strong will match all STRONG elements in the document. Opera 3 has much the same problem.

Examples

```
h1 + p {margin-top: 0;}
p+ul {margin-top: 0.5em; color: gray;}
p em + strong {font-style: italic;}
```

Attribute Selectors

An *attribute selector* is used to select elements based on the presence of certain attributes, or the values of attributes. There are four types of attribute selectors.

Generic Syntax

`X[attr]`

Selects any element X with the attribute `attr`.

X[attr="val"]

Selects any element X whose attribute `attr` has the value `val`. The match must be exact, so `[alt="Figure"]` will *not* match the `alt` value `Figure 1`. Spaces are permitted in the value.

X[attr~="val"]

Selects any element X whose attribute `attr` contains a space-separated list of values which includes `val`. Therefore, `[alt="Figure"]` will match the `alt` values `Figure 1`, `Great Figure`, `Figure this out`, and so forth.

X[attr|="val"]

Selects any element X whose attribute `attr` has a value which is a hyphen-separated list that begins with `val`. This is primarily intended to allow language matches; for example, the selector `[lang|="en"]` will match the values `en`, `en-us`, `en-uk`, and so on. It is possible to construct other matches, such as `[alt|="figure"]`. This would match the values `figure-1`, `figure-2`, and so on.

Notes

It is possible to combine more than one attribute selector within a single selector. For example, to select any anchor element which has the attributes `href` and `title`, the appropriate selector is `a[href][title]`. If the selector should match only those anchors with an `href` set to `http://www.w3.org/` and any `title` value, the correct selector is `a[title][href="http://www.w3.org/"]`.

Although they have a great many uses in relation to HTML and XHTML documents, attribute selectors are expected to see very heavy use with pure XML documents.

Opera 4 and 5 both incorrectly handle the `|=` attribute selector. They will match the specified value if it appears anywhere in the attribute; thus, `p[class|="three"]` will incorrectly match `<p class="bakers-three">`.

Examples

```
a[link] {color: blue;}
a[link="http://www.w3.org/"] {font-weight: bold;}
img[alt~="Figure"] {float: right;}
*[lang|="fr"] {font-style: italic;}
```

Class Selectors

For any element which has a `class` attribute, a *class selector* may be used to select on the value of the `class` attribute.

Generic Syntax

X.class1

Selects any element X whose `class` attribute has a value of `class1`.

X.class1.class2...

Selects any element X whose `class` attribute contains the space-separated values `class1` and `class2`, in any order. Any number of values may be chained together, so long as each is separated from the others by a period. Therefore, a selector such as `p.beach.hotel.rooms.rates` is a perfectly legitimate construct. There may be other space-separated values in the `class` attribute, and these will not interfere with the match. For example, `p.beach.hotel` would match the elements <p class="beach hotel rates"> and <p class="beach hotel pictures">, as well as the element <p class="hotel beach">.

.class1

Selects any element whose `class` attribute has a value of `class1`.

Notes

The class selector is a special HTML- and XHTML-specific notation, and uses a specific syntax which is relevant only to those languages. In those languages, the attribute `class` may appear on any element. Other markup languages may or may not permit this convention. For most XML-based languages, the attribute selectors will be more commonly used.

Under CSS1, classes could not start with a digit, but most browsers ignored this restriction. In CSS2, classes may begin with digits, so the original problem has in effect corrected itself.

Examples

```
p.warning .urgent {color; red; font-weight: bold;}
div.aside {border: 1px solid blue; background: silver;
  padding: 1em;}
.help {font-style: italic;}
```

ID selectors

An *ID selector* is very similar to the class selector.

Generic Syntax

`X#id1`

Selects any element X whose ID attribute has a value id1.

`#id1`

Selects any element whose ID attribute has a value id1.

Notes

Like the class selector, the ID selector is specific to HTML and XHTML. In this case, it is used to select values of the ID attribute, which may appear on any element. Note that HTML and XHTML restrict ID values to be unique within a given document; thus, there can only be one ID attribute with a value of jh8571 for each document. Other markup languages which permit the ID attribute may or may not enforce this uniqueness restriction.

Under CSS1, IDs could not start with a digit, but most browsers ignored this restriction. In CSS2, IDs may begin with digits, so the original problem has in effect corrected itself.

Examples

```
h1#page-title {border-bottom: 4px double gray;
  background: gray;}
div#zza77j {color: purple;}
#footer {border-top: 1px solid gray;}
```

Pseudo-Classes

A *pseudo-class* is a selector construct which causes a user agent to behave as though it has inserted "phantom classes" into the document markup, and then applied styles based on the modified markup. This is done in order to allow for styling based on things which do not appear in the document itself, such as the state of a hyperlink (e.g., visited or unvisited). Since this phantom markup is represented as a class-attribute structure, these constructs are referred to as pseudo-class selectors.

In CSS1, it was required that a pseudo-class selector be placed at the end of its associated selector. This led to the requirement that with class markup, the pseudo-class selector had to follow the class notation; e.g., `a.external:link`. This restriction was relaxed in CSS2 to allow the construction `a:link.warning`. However, this may not be recognized in older CSS-aware browsers, so it should be used with caution.

In CSS2, it is possible to chain multiple pseudo-class selectors together; for example, `a:link:hover` or `input:hover:focus`. This was not permitted under CSS1, and older CSS-aware browsers may ignore selectors which use this format, so it should be used with caution as well.

:first-child

The *:first-child selector* is used to select an element which is not only the child of another element, but is, in fact, the first child.

Generic Syntax

`X:first-child`

Selects any element X which is the first child of another element.

Notes

Any text which appears before the first child element will not affect the operation of this selector. For example, the selector `p.warning em:first-child` will match the first EM element in the following markup.

```
<p class="warning">This is warning text which
contains <em>some emphasized text</em> as well
as some <strong>strong text</strong>and
<em>more emphasized text</em>.
```

Again, only the first EM element will be selected, and the text which appears between the opening of the paragraph element and the beginning of the EM element does not prevent the selector from operating.

Examples

```
p:first-child {font-style: italic;}
ol li:first-child {text-indent: -2em;}
div:first-child em {font-weight: bold;}
```

:link

3

The *:link selector* is used to apply styles to any hyperlink which points to an unvisited resource.

Generic Syntax

`X:link`

Selects any element X which is a hyperlink and which points to an unvisited resource.

Notes

This link state is mutually exclusive with `:visited` (see the following section). Under HTML and XHTML, the only element which may take a `:link` pseudo-class is an anchor element (`A`) which has an `href` attribute. Other markup languages will almost certainly not have these restrictions, although they are likely to impose others.

Examples

```
a:link {color: blue; text-decoration: underline;}
a.external:link {color: olive;
   text-decoration: underline overline;}
```

:visited

The *:visited selector* is used to apply styles to any hyperlink which points to a visited resource.

Generic Syntax

`X:visited`

Selects any element X which is a hyperlink and which points to a resource which has been visited (e.g., one which appears in the browser's history list).

Notes

This state is mutually exclusive with :link (see earlier). Under HTML and XHTML, the only element which may take a :visited pseudo-class is an anchor element (a) which has an href attribute. Other markup languages will almost certainly not have these restrictions, although they are likely to impose others.

As the CSS specification says, user agents may choose to return a visited link to an unvisited state. It is up to each user agent to decide how long a link is treated as "visited" before reverting it to "unvisited" status.

Examples

```
a:visited {color: purple; text-decoration: none;}
a.external:visited {color: gray; font-weight: lighter;}
```

:hover

The *:hover selector* is used to apply styles to any element which has been designated in some way by the user.

Generic Syntax

X:hover
Selects any element X which is currently designated.

Notes

The most common method for "designating" an element without making it active is to move the mouse pointer (cursor) to a point within the element's box, so that the pointer appears to be "hovering over" the element.

There are no restrictions on the types of elements which can be selected, but most user agents apply :hover styles only to hyperlinks. :hover is not supported at all in Navigator 4.x, Opera 3, and Opera 4, even on hyperlinks.

:hover can be combined with other pseudo-classes to produce state-specific hover effects, but this syntax is not supported by older CSS-aware browsers.

Examples

```
p.example:hover {color: blue; background: yellow;}
a:link:hover {color: blue; background: silver;}
input:hover {color: maroon; background: yellow;}
```

:active

3

The *:active selector* is used to apply styles to any element which has been designated by the user and is currently active.

Generic Syntax

```
X:active
```

Selects any element X which is currently active.

Notes

The most common example of the "active" state is when the mouse pointer is positioned within (or "over") an element during the time in which the user is pressing down the mouse button. Although the most common way of making an element active is to "click on it" with the mouse, it is possible to designate the element via some other means (e.g., tabbing via the keyboard) and then select it through that same means (e.g., hitting the "return" key). Thus, it is possible for an element to be active without also being hovered.

There are no restrictions on the types of elements which can be selected, but most user agents apply :active styles to hyperlinks only. Navigator 4.x and Opera 3 do not support :active at all, even on hyperlinks.

:active can be combined with other pseudo-classes to produce state-specific hover effects, but this syntax is not supported by older CSS-aware browsers.

Examples

```
a:active {color: yellow; background: blue;}
a:link:active {color: white; background: black;}
a:visited:active {color: silver; background: gray;}
```

:focus

The *:focus selector* is used to apply styles to any element which currently has focus.

Generic Syntax

`X:focus`

Selects any element X which currently has focus.

Notes

The most common example of the focus state is a form element which is ready to accept keyboard input. There are no restrictions on the types of elements which can be selected, but many user agents apply `:focus` styles only to form elements, and sometimes to hyperlinks.

`:focus` can be combined with other pseudo-classes to produce state-specific hover effects, but this syntax is not supported by older CSS-aware browsers.

Examples

```
input:focus {color: black; background: yellow;}
a:focus:hover {font-weight: bold; outline: 1px solid red;}
select:focus {width: auto;}
```

:lang(n)

The *:lang selector* is used to apply styles to any element which is written in a specified language code, where the code is one specified by RFC 1766.

Generic Syntax

`X:lang(n)`

Selects any element X which uses the language *n*.

Notes

This selector operates in a fashion similar to the `|=` attribute selector, and is dependent on the document markup to provide the language information. In HTML and XHTML, this can be provided by means of the `lang` attribute on an element, a `meta` element within the document, or even in the HTTP headers of the document itself.

`:lang` can be combined with other pseudo-classes to produce state-specific hover effects, but this syntax is not supported by older CSS-aware browsers.

Examples

```
*:lang(fr) {font-weight: bold}
HTML:lang(de) {background: cyan;}
DIV:lang(en) {font-family: sans-serif;}
```

:left, :right, and :first

See Chapter 5, "Paged Media Styles."

Pseudo-Elements

A *pseudo-element* is a selector construct which causes a user agent to behave as though it has inserted phantom markup into a document, and then applied styles to that phantom element. This is done in order to allow for styling based on things which do not appear in the document itself, such as styling the first line of an element. Since this phantom markup is represented as an element-like structure, the constructs are called pseudo-element selectors.

In CSS, it is required that a pseudo-element selector be placed after the last selector in the overall selector (e.g., div ul ol.step strong:first-letter). Therefore, a pseudo-element selector must come after any pseudo-class selectors.

:first-letter

The *:first-letter selector* is used to apply styles to the first letter of an element.

Generic Syntax

X:first-letter
Applies styles to the first letter of any element X.

X.class1:first-letter
Applies styles to the first letter of any element X that has a CLASS attribute with a value of class1.

X#id1:first-letter
Applies styles to the first letter of any element X that has an ID attribute with a value of id1.

Notes

If the first letter is preceded by a punctuation mark, then the mark is styled along with the first letter. Note that only certain properties may be applied to a first letter.

Allowed Properties

The properties which may be used in a `:first-letter` rule are

font-variant	background	margin-top
font-style	float	margin-right
font-weight	clear	margin-bottom
font-size	vertical-align (if float is none)	margin-left
font-family	line-height	margin
font	text-decoration	padding-top
color	text-transform	padding-right
background-color	text-shadow	padding-bottom
background-image	word-spacing	padding-left
background-repeat	letter-spacing	padding

Examples

```
body:first-letter {font-style: italic;}
h1 + p:first-letter {font-size: 200%; color: red;
  float: left;}
*:first-child:first-letter {font-weight: bold;}
```

:first-line

The *:first-line selector* is used to apply styles to the first displayed line of an element.

Generic Syntax

X:first-line

Applies styles to the first displayed line of any element X.

X.class1:first-line

Applies styles to the first displayed line of any element X that has a `class` attribute with value `class1`.

`X#id1:first-line`

Applies styles to the first displayed line of any element X that has an `ID` attribute with value `id1`.

Notes

The actual text to which the styles are applied will change depending on the display environment, the styles used, and so on. Note that only certain properties may be applied to a first line.

Allowed Properties

The properties which may be used in a `:first-line` rule are

font-variant	background-color	text-decoration
font-style	background-image	text-transform
font-weight	background-repeat	text-shadow
font-size	background-attachment	word-spacing
font-family	background	letter-spacing
font	vertical-align	clear
color	line-height	

Examples

```
body:first-line {color: magenta;}
h1 + p:first-line {font-size: 200%; font-style: italic;}
*:first-child:first-line {font-weight: bold;}
```

:before

The *:before selector* is used to place generated content before the content of an element.

Generic Syntax

`X:before`

Causes content to be inserted into the displayed document immediately before the content of element X.

`X.class1:before`

Causes content to be inserted into the displayed document immediately before the content of element X that has an attribute `class` with a value of `class1`.

`X#id1:before`

Causes content to be inserted into the displayed document immediately before the content of element X that has an attribute ID with a value of `id1`.

Notes

This pseudo-element selector will insert into the displayed document content which does not appear in the markup. It is used in conjunction with the `content` property to specify exactly what is generated. Any styles which appear in the same rules will be applied to the generated content; in addition, any styles applied to the affected element which can be inherited will be inherited by the generated content. See the entry for `content` in Chapter 4, "Visual Media Styles," for more details.

Note that since this generated content does not appear in the document itself, it will not appear at all in older Web browsers, and will not be picked up by indexing programs. Thus, it is not recommended that necessary content be added in this manner.

Examples

```
h1.title:before {content: "Title: "; color: gray;}
blockquote:before {content: open-quote;}
p:before {content: url(paramark.gif);}
```

:after

The *:after selector* is used to place generated content after the content of an element.

Generic Syntax

`X:after`

Causes content to be inserted into the displayed document immediately after the content of element X.

`X.class1:after`

Causes content to be inserted into the displayed document immediately after the content of element X that has an attribute class with a value of `class1`.

`X#id1:after`

Causes content to be inserted into the displayed document immediately after the content of element X that has an attribute ID with a value of id1.

Notes

This pseudo-element inserts into the displayed document content which does not appear in the markup. It is used in conjunction with the `content` property to specify exactly what is generated. Any styles which appear in the same rules will be applied to the generated content; in addition, any styles applied to the affected element which can be inherited will be inherited by the generated content. See the entry for `content` in Chapter 4, "Visual Media Styles," for more details.

Note that since this generated content does not appear in the document itself, it will not appear at all in older Web browsers, and will not be picked up by indexing programs. Thus, it is not recommended that necessary content be added in this manner.

Examples

```
h1.title:after {content: "...";}
blockquote:after {content: close-quote;}
p:after {content: url(arrow.gif);}
```

At-Rules

An *at-rule* is a construct that begins with an "@" symbol immediately followed by an identifier. This identifier is then followed by a *block*, which is defined as all content contained within a set of curly braces ({ }); or else is followed by all content up until the next semicolon (;)—e.g., the syntax of the @import rule. Any unrecognized at-rule must be ignored in its entirety.

@import

The *@import rule* is used to associate an external stylesheet with the document.

Generic Syntax

```
@import url(...) <media>;
```

Components

url(...)

The `url(...)` portion of the rule contains the URL of the external stylesheet, with the actual URL replacing the `...` part. Both relative and absolute URLs are allowed, but only one URL may be included in each `@import` directive. This portion of the rule is *required*.

<media>

A comma-separated list of target media. This portion of the rule is optional.

Notes

An `@import` rule behaves in a fashion similar to the `LINK` element in HTML and XHTML, except that `@import` must appear either within a `STYLE` element or within an external stylesheet. Also, `@import` is language-independent; so long as CSS is recognized, `@import` can be used no matter what markup language is used to structure the actual content. Multiple `@import` rules are permitted within the same stylesheet, but all `@import` rules must appear before any other rules in the stylesheet, and may not appear inside other at-rule blocks. If an `@import` rule appears after other style rules in a stylesheet (e.g., `h1 {color: gray;}`), or is placed within another at-rule block, then CSS2 parsers are required to ignore the incorrectly placed `@import` rule.

By placing an `@import` rule inside an external stylesheet, it is possible to use one external stylesheet to bring in another. This sort of recursive importing of styles is not well supported in older browsers.

`@import` is not supported by Navigator 4.x, which is actually somewhat useful since it allows authors to "hide" styles which Navigator 4.x would have trouble interpreting. (For using external stylesheets in Navigator 4.x, see the entry on the `LINK` element in Chapter 1.)

Examples

```
<style type="text/css">
    @import url(http://www.my.site/styles/autumn.css);
</style>
<style type="text/css" media="screen,print">
```

```
    @import url(print-styles.css) print;
    P {margin-left: 1.25em;}
</style>
```

@media

The *@media rule* is used to specify the target media for a set of style rules. This permits the inclusion of styles for multiple media in a single stylesheet.

Generic Syntax
```
@media <media> {...styles...}
```

Components

<media>

The `<media>` portion is a comma-separated list of target media for the styles which follow. This portion of the rule is optional.

{...styles...}

The collection of rules which are to be applied in the target media. This portion of the rule is *required*.

Notes
Other rule blocks may not appear inside the `@media` rule block.

Examples
```
@media print {
    body {color: black; background; white;}
    a:link, a:visited {text-decoration: underline;}
}
@media screen, projection {
    body {color: black; background: #FCD;}
    a:link, a:visited {text-decoration: none;}
}
@media screen,print {
    * {line-height: 1.25;}
}
```

@charset

The *@charset rule* is used to specify the character encoding of a document.

Generic Syntax
```
@charset "<charset>";
```

Components

<charset>
This must be a character set as described in the IANA registry.

Notes
Only one `@charset` rule must appear in an external stylesheet, and it must be the very first thing in the stylesheet, with no content of any kind preceding it. `@charset` is not permitted in embedded stylesheets.

Examples
```
@charset "ISO-8859-1";
```

@font-face

The *@font-face* rule is used to exhaustively describe a font face for use in a document.

Generic Syntax
```
@font-face {<font-description>};
```

Components

<font-description>
This is formatted as a series of descriptor-value pairs.

Notes
`@font-face` may also be used to define the location of a font for download, although this may run into implementation-specific limits.

In general, `@font-face` is extremely complicated, and its use is not recommended for any except those who are expert in font metrics. A detailed exploration of `@font-face` could be a chapter (or even a book) in itself, and is not undertaken in this work. See the CSS2 specification, section 15.3, for more details.

Examples
```
@font-face {
font-family: "Scarborough Light";
```

```
      src: url("http://www.font.site/s/scarbo-lt");
}
@font-face {
      font-family: Santiago;
      src: local ("Santiago"),
           url("http://www.font.site/s/santiago.tt")
           format("truetype");
      unicode-range: U+??,U+100-220;
      font-size: all;
      font-family: sans-serif;
}
```

@page

See the entry for @page in Chapter 5, "Paged Media Styles," for details.

Chapter 4
Visual Media Styles

At its heart, CSS is a style language for visual presentation. Although it does have sections devoted to aural and paged media, the vast bulk of its properties and abilities lie in the visual realm. It is therefore unsurprising that the bulk of this reference should be devoted to explaining the visual media properties.

It is important to note that some of the properties in this section apply not only to visual media. Some of them are also used in the interactive medium, for example. Others, such as `display` and `position`, are used in non-visual media, but can have different effects in those media. These differences will be noted, and are also covered in the sections that address non-visual media.

It is important to note that in many circumstances "visual media" is just another term for "continuous media," which itself is a fancy way of saying "browser display." This isn't all the term "visual media" means, but it is what most people care about. Thus, there is a difference between visual and paged media, despite the fact that both are fundamentally dependent on vision to be comprehended. Paged media are covered in Chapter 5. For a review of the fundamentals of visual layout, refer to Chapter 1.

Although every property accepts `inherit` as a value, it is not discussed in detail in the following reference. The operation of `inherit` is discussed in Chapter 1, as it is the same for every property.

Reference

background

`background` is a shorthand element used to set background styles for an element.

Summary

Value Syntax
```
[<background-color> || <background-image> || <background-
repeat> || <background-attachment> || <background-position>] |
inherit
```

Initial Value
not defined for shorthand properties

Percentages
allowed on `<background-position>`

Inherited
no

Applies to
all elements

Media Groups
visual

Values

<background-color>
Sets a solid color for the element's background, padding, and border background. See the section on `background-color` for more details.

<background-image>
Defines the location of an image to be placed in the element's background. See the section on `background-image` for more details.

<background-repeat>
Sets a repeat direction for an image in the element's background. See the section on `background-repeat` for more details.

<background-attachment>
Sets an attachment state for any images in the element's background. See the section on `background-attachment` for more details.

<background-position>
Sets a position for the origin image in the element's background. See the section on `background-position` for more details.

Notes

Although all five background aspects can be set via background, only one of them is necessary to constitute a legal value. Thus, it is possible to set just the background color with background, thus returning the other four aspects to their default values. (See the section on shorthand properties in Chapter 1 for more details.)

In Navigator 4.x, background and its associated properties are not well supported. The most common problem is that a background applied to a block-level element will only set a background for the content of the element, not the entire background of the element. A workaround for this problem is to set an invisibly thin border around the element whose color matches the background of the parent element.

4

Examples

```
body {background: white url(/pix/sawtooth.gif) top center
    repeat-x scroll;}
table {background: silver;}
p.warning {background: yellow url(danger.jpg) repeat-y;}
```

Related Properties

background-attachment, background-color, background-image, background-position, background-repeat

background-attachment

background-attachment determines the tiling context and scroll state of a background image.

Summary

Value Syntax
scroll | fixed | inherit

Initial Value
scroll

Percentages
n/a

Inherited
no

Applies to
all elements

Media Groups
visual

Values

scroll
A background image set to `scroll` will scroll along with the rest of the document.

fixed
A background image set to `fixed` will remain locked in place while the rest of the document scrolls.

Notes

Although it seems simple in concept, `background-attachment` is actually quite powerful and in some ways very complicated.

If a background image is set to be `fixed`, it is locked in place and cannot move while the rest of the document scrolls. One way to take advantage of this effect is to define a tiled pattern which is the same size as a tiled pattern in the background, but a different color. For example, consider:

```
body {background: green url(greentile.gif) fixed;}
h1 {background: blue url(bluetile.gif) fixed;}
```

For this example, we'll assume that the two background images are the same color. Since the tiling context for both elements is the top left corner of the document, the tiled backgrounds will line up with each other. As the H1 element scrolls around the screen, it will "look into" different parts of its own background, which will always be lined up with the body's background. Thus, it will appear to change the color of the tiled background.

There is a potential danger with this property, however. Since fixed backgrounds are positioned with respect to the viewport, they may be placed outside the background and padding of the element to which they belong. In order to understand this, consider the following rule:

```
h2 {background: black url(star.jpg) center fixed no-repeat;}
```

Here we have a single image which will be centered in viewport, will not be tiled, and will not scroll with the document. However, there is no guarantee that an H2 element will be placed at the center of the viewport. In that case, the background image will not be visible, since it is placed outside the padding and background of the H2. Only when an H2 is at the center of the viewport will the associated background image be visible. In addition, if multiple rules place different background images in the same position (the center of the document), they will overlap in some sense. However, since elements do not generally overlap, this is not necessarily a problem. As each element scrolls past the center of the viewport, it will reveal some or all of its associated background image.

However, only Navigator 6 and Internet Explorer 5 for Macintosh support this behavior. All other known browsers support fixed backgrounds on the BODY element in HTML, but do not support the "alignment" behavior described.

The specification allows user agents to treat fixed as scroll. This has the same effect as not supporting background-attachment at all, since all known visual browsers implement the background-scrolling behavior as part of their HTML handling.

Examples
```
body {background-attachment: fixed;}
h1 {background-attachment: scroll;}
```

Related Properties
```
background, background-color, background-image,
background-position, background-repeat
```

background-color

background-color sets a solid color for the entire background, including the padding and border background, of an element.

Summary
Value Syntax
```
<color> | transparent | inherit
```

Initial Value
```
transparent
```

Percentages
n/a

Inherited
no

Applies to
all elements

Media Groups
visual

Values

<color>
Any color value (see the section on color units in Chapter 2 for more details).

transparent
Allows the backgrounds of ancestor elements to "shine through," or be visible behind this element.

Notes
Although the default value of transparent is honored by all known browsers, explicitly setting a value of transparent in Navigator 4.x will result in a black background. In a related bug, setting the value to inherit will result in a sickly green.

Examples
```
body {background-color: white;}
h1 {background-color: rgb(100%,60%,33.33%);}
p.warning {background-color: #FF0;}
```

Related Properties
background, background-attachment, background-image, background-position, background-repeat

background-image

background-image defines a pointer to an image resource which is to be placed in the background of an element.

Summary

Value Syntax
<uri> | none | inherit

Initial Value
none

Percentages
n/a

Inherited
no

Applies to
all elements

Media Groups
visual

Values

<uri>
The user agent should use the image defined by that URI as the background image. If the URI points to something other than an image, then it is to be ignored and the user agent should act as though background-image had been set to none.

none
Setting background-image to none means that no background image should be used for matching elements.

Notes

By default, background images are tiled from the top left corner of the element and will scroll with the document; however, all this can be changed via other background properties. If an image cannot be found, or if portions of the image are transparent, then the background color of the element "fills in" the blank parts. If the background color is transparent, then the backgrounds of any ancestor elements will be visible through the blank parts. Background images with alpha channels, such as those in the PNG format, should composite the image with the color provided by `background-color`, and with the background of any ancestor elements which are visible.

It is generally a good practice to make sure that a background color is set along with a background image, especially if the foreground (text) color is meant to be complemented by the background color. By providing a background color as a fallback, authors can do their best to ensure that the document will be readable even if the background image cannot be displayed for some reason.

Examples

```
body {background-image: url(http://www.images.net/cat1/newts.gif);}
table {background-image: url(wavy.jpg);}
pre {background-image: none;}
```

Related Properties

`background`, `background-attachment`, `background-color`, `background-position`, `background-repeat`

background-position

`background-position` determines the placement of the origin element; that is, the point from which a repeated background begins.

Summary

Value Syntax
`[ [<percentage> | <length> ]{1,2} | [ [top | center | bottom] || [left | center | right] ] ] | inherit`

Initial Value
`0% 0%`

Percentages
refer to the size of the box itself

Inherited
no

Applies to
block-level and replaced elements

Media Groups
visual

Values

percentage
Causes the appropriate point within the origin image to be aligned with the appropriate point in the background of the element. The percentage values are used to calculate both points. If one percentage value is given, it is used for both horizontal and vertical axes. If two values are given, the first is used for the horizontal axis, and the second for the vertical. Thus, for a value of 50% 50%, the middle of the origin image is aligned with the middle of the background; for a value of 100% 100%, the bottom right corner of the origin image aligns with the bottom right corner of the element background. Percentage values may not be mixed with keywords such as left, but may be mixed with length values.

<length>
Defines the offset of the top left corner of the origin image from the top left corner of the background. If one length value is given, it is used for both horizontal and vertical axes. If two values are given, the first is used for the horizontal axis, and the second for the vertical. Length values may be mixed with percentage values, but not with keywords such as top.

top
Causes the top edge of the origin image to be aligned with the top edge of the background. top may be used in conjunction with the keywords left, center, and right. If it is used by itself, top is equivalent to the value 50% 0%.

bottom
Causes the bottom edge of the origin image to be aligned with the bottom edge of the background. bottom may be used in conjunction with the keywords left, center, and right. If it is used by itself, bottom is equivalent to the value 50% 100%.

left
Causes the left edge of the origin image to be aligned with the left edge of the background. left may be used in conjunction with the keywords top, center, and bottom. If it is used by itself, left is equivalent to the value 0% 50%.

right
Causes the right edge of the origin image to be aligned with the right edge of the background. right may be used in conjunction with the keywords top, center, and bottom. If it is used by itself, right is equivalent to the value 100% 50%.

center

Causes the center of the origin image to be aligned with the center of at least one axis of the background. center may be used in conjunction with any of the keywords. If it is used by itself, center is equivalent to the value 50% 50% (and is also equivalent to center center).

Notes

The term *origin image* is a condensed way of saying "place from which the tiling of the background image will commence." By default, a background image is repeated in all four directions—up, down, right, and left—infinitely. (See background-repeat for information on how to alter this behavior.) Changing the position of the origin image can change the way the background is laid out. For example, a grid-pattern will look quite different if it tiles from the center of the background, instead of from the top left corner. This difference will be seen primarily around the edges of the element's background, where the clipping of the background will change depending on the origin image's placement.

If a length unit and a percentage are used together, or if two length or two percentage values are specified, then the first is used for the horizontal axis, and the second for the vertical. Length and percentage values may be negative, and will push the origin image above and to the left of the top left corner of the element's box. However, there may be unexpected results, as user agents are not required to support this behavior.

Keyword combinations may occur in any order, thanks to their inherent meanings. Thus, top left and left top will have the same effect, and both are equivalent to the value 0% 0%.

Navigator 4.x does not support background-position at all.

Examples

```
body {background-position: top center;}
h1 {background-position: 50%;}
td.sidebar {background-position: -10px 33%;}
```

Related Properties

background, background-attachment, background-color, background-image, background-repeat

background-repeat

`background-repeat` defines the directions in which a background image will be repeated (if any).

Summary

Value Syntax
repeat | repeat-x | repeat-y | no-repeat | inherit

Initial Value
repeat

Percentages
n/a

Inherited
no

Applies to
all elements

Media Groups
visual

Values

repeat
Causes the background image to be repeated along both the horizontal and vertical axes. This is the "tiling" effect familiar from traditional HTML browsers.

repeat-x
Causes the background image to be repeated along the x axis. Note that this means it will repeat to both the right *and* left, not just to the right.

repeat-y
Causes the background image to be repeated along the y axis. Note that this means it will repeat to both up *and* down, not just down.

no-repeat
Prevents the background image from being repeated at all. The origin image will be placed in the background, but no "tiling" will occur.

Notes

The tiling effects of `background-repeat` are often misunderstood by authors. The common assumption is that once the origin image has been placed via `background-position`, the background will repeat down and to the right. Were this true, then centering the origin image and setting `background-repeat` to `repeat` would fill the background into the lower right quadrant of the background. Instead, the background will fill the entire background, as an author would expect.

This allows authors to center an image and repeat it along one axis or another. Assume a sine-wave pattern image which describes a single sine. This can be set as a background image, the origin image moved to the center of the element's background, and the repetition set to `repeat-x`. This will cause the sine wave to stretch from one side of the background to the other, with the entire series of waves centered within the element.

Internet Explorer 4 for Windows repeats backgrounds only down and to the right, not in both directions along the axes.

Examples

```
body {background-image: url(sideteeth.png);
   background-repeat: repeat-y;}
h1 {background-image: url(sinewave.gif);
   background-repeat: repeat-x;}
table {background-repeat: repeat;}
```

Related Properties

`background`, `background-attachment`, `background-color`, `background-image`, `background-position`

border

`border` is a shorthand property which sets the style, color, and width of the border around an element.

Summary

Value Syntax
[<border-width> || <border-style> || <color>] | inherit

Initial Value
not defined for shorthand properties

Percentages
n/a

Inherited
no

Applies to
all elements

Media Groups
visual

Values

<border-width>
Any length value, or one of the keywords `thin,` `medium,` and `thick` (see `border-width` for more details). This sets the width for the border around the entire element. Length values for border widths may not be negative.

<border-style>
Any permitted border style (see `border-style` for more details). This sets the style for the border around the entire element.

<color>
Any color value (see the section on color units in Chapter 2 for more details). This sets the color for the border around the entire element.

Notes
Since this property can only accept a single keyword for each aspect (style, color, and width), use of `border` is generally restricted to those cases in which an author wishes to set a consistent border all the way around an element. In addition, since it is a shorthand property, its values can override those set by earlier rules; see the section on shorthand properties in Chapter 1 for more details.

Examples
```
pre {border: thin solid purple;}
p.warning {border: 0.25em double red;}
a:link img {border: 2px solid blue;}
```

Related Properties
border-bottom, border-color, border-left, border-top, border-right, border-style, border-width

border-bottom

`border-bottom` is a shorthand property which sets the style, color, and width of the bottom border of an element.

Summary

Value Syntax
[`<border-bottom-width>` || `<border-style>` || `<color>`] | `inherit`

Initial Value
not defined for shorthand properties

Percentages
n/a

Inherited
no

Applies to
all elements

Media Groups
visual

Values

\<border-bottom-width\>
Any length value, or one of the keywords `thin`, `medium`, and `thick` (see `border-width` for more details). Length values for border widths may not be negative.

\<border-style\>
Any permitted value for the property `border-style`.

\<color\>
Any color value (see the section on color units in Chapter 2 for more details). If no color is specified by this property or another border property, then the foreground color of the element is used for the border's color.

Notes

Note that if no border style is supplied, then the border will not exist (see `border-style` for more details).

Examples

```
h1 {border-bottom: 0.25em double gray;}
a {border-bottom: 1px solid;}
pre {border-bottom: thin outset rgb(25%, 75%, 42.13%);}
```

Related Properties

`border`, `border-bottom-color`, `border-bottom-style`, `border-bottom-width`, `color`

border-bottom-color

`border-bottom-color` sets the color of the bottom border of an element.

Summary

Value Syntax
`<color> | inherit`

Initial Value
the value of the `color` property for the element

Percentages
n/a

Inherited
no

Applies to
all elements

Media Groups
visual

Values

<color>
Any color value (see the section on color units in Chapter 2 for more details). If no color is specified by this property or another border property, then the foreground color of the element is used for the border's color.

Notes

Since this property sets the color for a single side of the border, it can only accept one color value.

Examples

```
h2 {border-bottom-color: purple;}
table {border-bottom-color: #C0A467;}
```

Related Properties

border, border-bottom, border-bottom-style,
border-bottom-width, border-color, color

border-bottom-style

border-bottom-style sets the style of the bottom border of
an element.

Summary

Value Syntax
<border-style> | inherit

Initial Value
none

Percentages
n/a

Inherited
no

Applies to
all elements

Media Groups
visual

Values

<border-style>
Any permitted value of the property border-style.

Notes

The default value of none will cause the border to have no existence,
and therefore no width (see border-style for more details).

Examples

```
h4 {border-bottom-style: inset;}
ol {border-bottom-style: none;}
```

Related Properties
border, border-bottom, border-bottom-color,
border-bottom-width, border-style

border-bottom-width

border-bottom-width sets the width of the bottom border of
an element.

Summary

Value Syntax
<border-width> | inherit

Initial Value
medium

Percentages
n/a

Inherited
no

Applies to
all elements

Media Groups
visual

Values

<border-width>
Any length value, or one of the keywords thin, medium, and thick
(see border-width for more details). Length values for this property
may not be negative.

Notes

The value provided for border-bottom-width will only have an
effect if a border style other than none has been set for the bottom
border (see border-style for more details). If the style of the
bottom border is set to none, whether via border-bottom-style,
border-style, or border, then the width of the border is reset to 0.

Examples

```
p.footer {border-bottom-width: 1px;}
h1 {border-bottom-width: 0.125em;}
```

Related Properties

`border`, `border-bottom`, `border-bottom-color`,
`border-bottom-style`, `border-width`

border-collapse

`border-collapse` determines the border model used in the
rendering of a table.

Summary

Value Syntax
collapse | separate | inherit

Initial Value
collapse

Percentages
n/a

Inherited
yes

Applies to
elements with a `display` of `table` or `inline-table`

Media Groups
visual

Values

collapse
Sets a table to use a collapsing-border method of layout. With this
method, two adjacent cells will share a border between them, with
the border chosen depending on a number of rules.

   1. Borders with a border-style of hidden will suppress any border
      at that location. Thus, setting the first table cell in a row to
      `border-style: groove` and then setting the style of the
      second cell in the row to `border-left-style: hidden` will
      eliminate the grooved border the two cells might otherwise
      have shared. The visual effect will be the same as if the two

cells were merged into one cell, although the top and bottom borders of the first cell will not extend to the second cell.

2. A `border-style` of `none` has the lowest priority, in terms of determining which border style should be used for a given shared border. Thus, if two adjacent cells have styles of `solid` and `none`, respectively, then the cell set to solid will have a solid border around its entire perimeter.

3. Narrow borders are discarded in favor of wider borders. This rule is ignored if any of the adjacent borders has a `border-style` of `hidden`, or if any of them is set to `none`.

4. If adjacent borders have the same width, then the `border-style` to be used is chosen in the order of preference `double`, `solid`, `dashed`, `dotted`, `ridge`, `outset`, `groove`, and last, `inset`.

5. If adjacent borders are the same style and width, but different colors, then the border to be used is chosen in the order of preference cell, row, row group, column, column group, and last, table.

Although the process sounds quite convoluted, this method is in fact the same as that used by traditional HTML browsers. Under this method, groups of cells (i.e., columns and rows) can have borders. If the `border-collapse: collapse` is declared for a given table, then `empty-cells` and `border-spacing` should be ignored within that table.

separate
Sets a table to use a separate-border method of layout. Under this method, every cell has its own border, and none of these borders are shared with other cells in the table. The gaps between the cells (if any) are set using the property `border-spacing`, and any blank space between cells is filled with the table's background. When using this method only cells may be assigned. If `border-collapse: separate` is declared for a given table, then any border styles declared for rows, columns, and groups of table elements within that table will be ignored. Furthermore, the rendering of empty cells is controlled by the property `empty-cells`.

Notes
As of this writing, support for table rendering with CSS was almost non-existent. Thus, browsers effectively supported `border-collapse: collapse`, which means that `border-spacing` and `empty-cells` had no effect.

Examples

```
table.old-style {border-collapse: collapse;}
table.spacious {border-collapse: separate;}
```

Related Properties

```
border-spacing, empty-cells
```

border-color

```
border-color
```
 is a shorthand property used to set the color of all four border sides of an element.

Summary

Value Syntax
```
<color>{1,4} | transparent | inherit
```

Initial Value
not defined for shorthand properties

Percentages
n/a

Inherited
no

Applies to
all elements

Media Groups
visual

Values

<color>
Any color value (see the section on color units in Chapter 2 for more details). If there are four color values declared, they apply in the order: top, right, bottom, left. In the case of three color values, the first will apply to the top border, the second to the left and right borders, and the third to the bottom border. If two color values are declared, the first applies to the top and bottom borders, while the second applies to the left and right borders. If one color value is declared, it applies to all four sides.

transparent

Sets the border to be invisible. In this state, the border may still have width, but it will not be drawn. This is similar to setting the property `border-style` to be `hidden`, except that in this case the element's border style is not affected. This keyword must be used alone, and will thus set all four border sides to be invisible.

Notes

Some border styles may alter the color from what is declared. For example, the `inset` and `outset` border styles use "highlight" and "shaded" variants of the declared color to give the impression of the element being raised from (or depressed into) the document.

Examples

```
h1 {border-color: #000000 gray;}
p.warning {border-color: rgb(255,0,0);}
div.circus {border-color: green red magenta yellow;}
```

Related Properties

`border`, `border-bottom-color`, `border-left-color`, `border-right-color`, `border-top-color`, `color`

border-left

`border-left` is a shorthand property which sets the style, color, and width of the left border of an element.

Summary

Value Syntax
[<border-left-width> || <border-style> || <color>] | inherit

Initial Value
not defined for shorthand properties

Percentages
n/a

Inherited
no

Applies to
all elements

Media Groups
visual

Values

<border-left-width>
Any length value, or one of the keywords thin, medium, and thick
(see border-width for more details). Length values for border widths
may not be negative.

<border-style>
Any permitted value for the property border-style.

<color>
Any color value (see the section on color units in Chapter 2 for
more details). If no color is specified by this property or another
border property, then the foreground color of the element is used
for the border's color.

Notes

Note that if no border style is supplied, then the border will not
exist (see border-style for more details).

Examples

```
h1 {border-left: 0.25em double gray;}
a {border-left: 1px solid;}
pre {border-left: thin outset rgb(25%, 75%, 42.13%);}
```

Related Properties

border, border-left-color, border-left-style,
border-left-width, color

border-left-color

border-left-color sets the color of the left border of an element.

Summary

Value Syntax
<color> | inherit

Initial Value
the value of the color property for the element

Percentages
n/a

Inherited
no

Applies to
all elements

Media Groups
visual

Values

<color>
Any color value (see the section on color units in Chapter 2 for more details). If no color is specified by this property or another border property, then the foreground color of the element is used for the border's color.

Notes
Since this property sets the color for a single side of the border, it can only accept one color value.

Examples
```
h2 {border-left-color: purple;}
table {border-left-color: #C0A467;}
```

Related Properties
border, border-left, border-left-style, border-left-width, border-color, color

border-left-style

border-left-style sets the style of the left border of an element.

Summary

Value Syntax
<border-style> | inherit

Initial Value
none

Percentages
n/a

Inherited
no

Applies to
all elements

Media Groups
visual

Values

<border-style>
Any permitted value of the property `border-style`.

Notes

The default value of `none` will cause the border to have no existence, and therefore no width (see `border-style` for more details).

Examples

```
h4 {border-left-style: inset;}
ol {border-left-style: none;}
```

Related Properties

`border, border-left, border-left-color, border-left-width, border-style`

border-left-width

`border-left-width` sets the width of the left border of an element.

Summary

Value Syntax
`<border-width> | inherit`

Initial Value
medium

Percentages
n/a

Inherited
no

Applies to
all elements

Media Groups
visual

Values

<border-width>
Any length value, or one of the keywords thin, medium, and thick (see border-width for more details). Length values for this property may not be negative.

Notes

The value provided for border-left-width will only have an effect if a border style other than none has been set for the left border (see border-style for more details). If the style of the left border is set to none, whether via border-left-style, border-style, or border, then the width of the border is reset to 0.

Examples

```
p.footer (border-left-width: 1px;}
h1 {border-left-width: 0.125em;}
```

Related Properties

border, border-left, border-left-color,
border-left-style, border-width

border-right

border-right is a shorthand property which sets the style, color, and width of the right border of an element.

Summary

Value Syntax
[<border-right-width> || <border-style> ||
<color>] | inherit

Initial Value
not defined for shorthand properties

Percentages
n/a

Inherited
no

Applies to
all elements

Media Groups
visual

Values

<border-right-width>
Any length value, or one of the keywords thin, medium, and thick
(see border-width for more details). Length values for border
widths may not be negative.

<border-style>
Any permitted value for the property border-style.

<color>
Any color value (see the section on color units in Chapter 2 for
more details). If no color is specified by this property or another
border property, then the foreground color of the element is used
for the border's color.

Notes
Note that if no border style is supplied, then the border will not
exist (see border-style for more details).

Examples
```
h1 {border-right: 0.25em double gray;}
a {border-right: 1px solid;}
pre {border-right: thin outset rgb(25%, 75%, 42.13%);}
```

Related Properties
border, border-right-color, border-right-style,
border-right-width, color

border-right-color

border-right-color sets the color of the right border of
an element.

Summary

Value Syntax
<color> | inherit

Initial Value
the value of the color property for the element

Percentages
n/a

Inherited
no

Applies to
all elements

Media Groups
visual

Values

<color>
Any color value (see the section on color units in Chapter 2 for more details). If no color is specified by this property or another border property, then the foreground color of the element is used for the border's color.

Notes

Since this property sets the color for a single side of the border, it can only accept one color value.

Examples

```
h2 {border-right-color: purple;}
table {border-right-color: #C0A467;}
```

Related Properties

border, border-right, border-right-style, border-right-width, border-color, color

border-right-style

border-right-style sets the style of the right border of an element.

Summary

Value Syntax
<border-style> | inherit

Initial Value
none

Percentages
n/a

Inherited
no

Applies to
all elements

Media Groups
visual

Values

<border-style>
Any permitted value of the property border-style.

Notes
The default value of none will cause the border to have no existence, and therefore no width (see border-style for more details).

Examples
h4 {border-right-style: inset;}
ol {border-right-style: none;}

Related Properties
border, border-right, border-right-color, border-right-width, border-style

border-right-width

border-right-width sets the width of the right border of an element.

Summary

Value Syntax
<border-width> | inherit

Initial Value
medium

Percentages
n/a

Inherited
no

Applies to
all elements

Media Groups
visual

Values

<border-width>
Any length value, or one of the keywords thin, medium, and thick
(see border-width for more details). Length values for this property
may not be negative.

Notes
The value provided for border-right-width will only have an
effect if a border style other than none has been set for the right
border (see border-style for more details). If the style of the
right border is set to none, whether via border-right-style,
border-style, or border, then the width of the border is reset
to 0.

Examples
p.footer (border-right-width: 1px;}
h1 {border-right-width: 0.125em;}

Related Properties
border, border-right, border-right-color,
border-right-style, border-width

border-spacing

border-spacing sets the distance between cells in a table, assuming
that the table is rendered using the separate-borders model.

Summary

Value Syntax
`<length> <length>? | inherit`

Initial Value
`0`

Percentages
n/a

Inherited
yes

Applies to
elements with a `display` of `table` or `inline-table`

Media Groups
visual

Values

\<length>
Any length unit. If two values are declared, the first applies to spacing along the horizontal axis, and the second applies to the vertical axis. If one value is declared, it applies to both axes. Length values for this property may not be negative.

Notes

If the property `border-collapse` is set to `collapse` (its default value), any value declared for `border-spacing` will be ignored.

Examples

```
table {border-collapse: separate; border-spacing: 1px;}
table.widen {border-collapse: separate; border-spacing: 0.5in;}
```

Related Properties

`border-collapse`, `empty-cells`

border-style

`border-style` is a shorthand property used to set the styles of the four border sides of an element.

Summary

Value Syntax
[none | hidden | dotted | dashed | solid | double |
groove | ridge | inset | outset]{1,4} | inherit

Initial Value
not defined for shorthand properties

Percentages
n/a

Inherited
no

Applies to
all elements

Media Groups
visual

4

Values

none
No border is drawn. The primary side effect of this value is that the computed border-width for the border in question will be set to 0.

hidden
Equivalent to none, except in the context of tables which are rendered with the collapsed-border model (see border-collapse for more details). This value cannot be used in conjunction with outlines (see outline-style for more details).

dotted
The border is drawn as a series of dots. The specific placement of these dots is left to the user agent.

dashed
The border is drawn as a series of short line segments. The specific placement of these lines is left to the user agent.

solid
The border is drawn as a single unbroken line.

double
The border is drawn as a pair of unbroken lines. The specific placement of these lines, including the separation between them, is left
to the user agent.

groove
The border is drawn as though it were a furrow carved into the
surface of the document. This implies a "shading" of the border,
but the CSS specification does not describe this in detail. Most
user agents handle this shading by splitting each border into two
adjacent lines, and darkening the upper (or leftward) half while
lightening the lower (or rightward) half of each border.

ridge
The border is drawn as though it were a ridge pushing up the
surface of the document. This implies a "shading" of the border,
but the CSS specification does not describe this in detail. Most
user agents handle this shading by splitting each border into two
adjacent lines, and lightening the upper (or leftward) half while
darkening the lower (or rightward) half of each border.

inset
The border is drawn as though the entire element is pushing the
surface of the document away from the user. This implies a "shading"
of the border, but the CSS specification does not describe this in
detail. Most user agents handle this shading by lightening the
bottom and right borders while darkening the top and left borders.

outset
The border is drawn as though the entire element is pushing the
surface of the document toward the user. This implies a "shading"
of the border, but the CSS specification does not describe this in
detail. Most user agents handle this shading by darkening the
bottom and right borders while lightening the top and left borders.

Notes

If there are four style values declared, they apply in the order: top,
right, bottom, left. In the case of three style values, the first will
apply to the top border, the second to the left and right borders,
and the third to the bottom border. If two style values are declared,
the first applies to the top and bottom borders, while the second
applies to the left and right borders. If one style value is declared,
it applies to all four sides.

In the case of those border styles which have gaps (dotted,
dashed, and double), the background of the element should

be visible through the gaps. In other words, the border is always drawn on top of the element's background, which ends at the outer edge of the border.

In the case of those border styles which require shading (`groove`, `ridge`, `inset`, and `outset`), the actual shaded colors used are based on the value of `border-color` for that border. It may also be altered by any background which is visible behind the border, although, as of this writing, this behavior has not been implemented.

User agents are permitted to interpret `dotted`, `dashed`, `double`, `groove`, `ridge`, `inset`, and `outset` as `solid`. Navigator 4.x does just that.

The keywords permitted for this property collectively make up the `<border-style>` value group.

4

Examples

```
h3 {border-style: ridge none;}
pre {border-style: inset;}
div.crazy {border-style: double dotted outset solid;}
img {border-style: outset;}
```

Related Properties

`border`, `border-bottom-style`, `border-left-style`, `border-right-style`, `border-top-style`

border-top

`border-top` is a shorthand property which sets the style, color, and width of the top border of an element.

Summary

Value Syntax
[`<border-top-width>` || `<border-style>` || `<color>`] | `inherit`

Initial Value
not defined for shorthand properties

Percentages
n/a

Inherited
no

Applies to
all elements

Media Groups
visual

Values

<border-top-width>
Any length value, or one of the keywords thin, medium, and thick (see border-width for more details). Length values for border widths may not be negative.

<border-style>
Any permitted value for the property border-style.

<color>
Any color value (see the section on color units in Chapter 2 for more details). If no color is specified by this property or another border property, then the foreground color of the element is used for the border's color.

Notes
Note that if no border style is supplied, then the border will not exist (see border-style for more details).

Examples
```
h1 {border-top: 0.25em double gray;}
a {border-top: 1px solid;}
pre {border-top: thin outset rgb(25%, 75%, 42.13%);}
```

Related Properties
border, border-top-color, border-top-style, border-top-width, color

border-top-color

border-top-color sets the color of the top border of an element.

Summary

Value Syntax
<color> | inherit

Initial Value
the value of the `color` property for the element

Percentages
n/a

Inherited
no

Applies to
all elements

Media Groups
visual

Values

<color>
Any color value (see the section on color units in Chapter 2 for more details). If no color is specified by this property or another border property, then the foreground color of the element is used for the border's color.

Notes

Since this property sets the color for a single side of the border, it can only accept one color value.

Examples

```
h2 {border-top-color: purple;}
table {border-top-color: #C0A467;}
```

Related Properties

border, border-top, border-top-style, border-top-width, border-color, color

border-top-style

`border-top-style` sets the style of the top border of an element.

Summary

Value Syntax
<border-style> | inherit

Initial Value
none

Percentages
n/a

Inherited
no

Applies to
all elements

Media Groups
visual

Values

<border-style>
Any permitted value of the property border-style.

Notes

The default value of none will cause the border to have no existence, and therefore no width (see border-style for more details).

Examples

```
h4 {border-top-style: inset;}
ol {border-top-style: none;}
```

Related Properties

border, border-top, border-top-color,
border-top-width, border-style

border-top-width

border-top-width sets the width of the top border of an element.

Summary

Value Syntax
<border-width> | inherit

Initial Value
medium

Percentages
n/a

Inherited
no

Applies to
all elements

Media Groups
visual

Values

<border-width>
Any length value, or one of the keywords thin, medium, and thick (see border-width for more details). Length values for this property may not be negative.

Notes
The value provided for border-top-width will only have an effect if a border style other than none has been set for the top border (see border-style for more details). If the style of the top border is set to none, whether via border-top-style, border-style, or border, then the width of the border is reset to 0.

Examples
p.footer (border-top-width: 1px;}
h1 {border-top-width: 0.125em;}

Related Properties
border, border-top, border-top-color,
border-top-style, border-width

border-width

border-width is a shorthand property used to set the width of the four border sides of an element.

Summary

Value Syntax
```
[ <length> | thin | medium | thick ]{1,4} | inherit
```

Initial Value
not defined for shorthand properties

Percentages
n/a

Inherited
no

Applies to
all elements

Media Groups
visual

Values

<length>
Any length unit. Length units for this property may not be negative.

thin
A border which is thinner than a border set to `medium`. The exact width is not defined by the CSS specification.

medium
A border which is thicker than a border set to `thin`, and thinner than a border set to `thick`. The exact width is not defined by the CSS specification.

thick
A border which is thicker than a border set to `medium`. The exact width is not defined by the CSS specification.

Notes

Length and keyword values may be mixed together. If there are four values declared, they apply in the order: top, right, bottom, left. In the case of three values, the first will apply to the top border, the second to the left and right borders, and the third to the bottom border. If two values are declared, the first applies to the top and bottom borders, while the second applies to the left and right borders. If one value is declared, it applies to all four sides.

Note that a border's width will be reset to 0 if the value of the property border-style is none.

Examples
```
p.aside {border-width: 1em;}
ul {border-width: thick 1px;}
h2 {border-width: 0.66ex thin 1mm;}
```

Related Properties
border, border-bottom-width, border-left-width, border-right-width, border-top-width

4

bottom

bottom defines an offset of the bottom edge of an absolutely positioned element from the bottom edge of its positioning context, or the vertical distance which a relatively positioned element will be displaced.

Summary

Value Syntax
<length> | <percentage> | auto | inherit

Initial Value
auto

Percentages
refer to height of containing block

Inherited
no

Applies to
positioned elements

Media Groups
visual

Values

<length>
A fixed distance from the bottom of the positioning context.

\<percentage\>

Some percentage of the height of the positioning context, assuming
that the height of the context has been set explicitly. If not, then
a percentage value for `bottom` is treated as though it were `auto`.
In practice, this means that percentage values for `bottom` set on
relatively positioned elements will be ignored.

auto

The actual distance which results will depend on a number of factors.
These factors are the dimensions of vertical measure for an absolutely
positioned element (see the notes section). If the element has been
relatively positioned, then `auto` has no apparent effect.

Notes

In the case of an absolutely positioned element, the vertical
dimensions of the element must add up to the height of the
positioning context. If every measure of vertical distance besides
`bottom` is explicitly set, then a value of `auto` is changed to make
sure that they all add up to the height of the positioning context.
Similarly, if all of the vertical dimensions including `bottom` are
explicitly set, but do not add up to the height of the positioning
context, then the value for `bottom` is discarded, and the necessary
value is substituted. In both cases, a negative distance may be
assigned to `bottom`. In addition, setting `bottom` to `auto` may force
other vertical dimensions which are also set to `auto` to be reset to
0. See the section on positioning calculations in Chapter 1 for more
information.

In the case of relatively positioned elements, `bottom` defines a vertical
offset from the place where the relatively positioned element would
ordinarily have appeared. Positive values for `bottom` will offset the
element upward, and negative values will move it downward. If
both `top` and `bottom` are set to explicit values, then the value for
`bottom` will be discarded in favor of `top`.

Examples

```
div.sidebar {position: absolute; width: 90%; margin: 0; padding: 0;
   height: auto; bottom: 13%;}
sub {vertical-align: baseline; position: relative; bottom: -0.5em;}
```

Related Properties

`height`, `left`, `position`, `right`, `top`

caption-side

`caption-side` determines the placement of the element box of a table's caption.

Summary

Value Syntax
top | bottom | left | right | inherit

Initial Value
top

Percentages
n/a

Inherited
yes

Applies to
elements with a `display` of `table-caption`

Media Groups
visual

Values

top
Places the caption's element box above the table box. The element box will be treated as a block-level box immediately preceding the table, with two exceptions. First, the caption will inherit styles from the table, and any ancestor elements within the table. Second, the caption is not considered to be a block-level element for the purposes of any element which precedes the table and has a `display` of either `compact` or `run-in`. The element box is treated as a block-level element for the purposes of width calculations, although these are done with the table's element box as the parent.

bottom
Places the caption's element box below the table box. Much as with `caption-side: top`, the element box will be treated as a block-level box which immediately follows the table, will inherit styles from the table, and has its width calculated with respect to the table's element box.

left

Places the caption's element box to the left of the table box. The width of this caption may be explicitly set; or, if set to `auto`, will be determined by the user agent. The caption may be aligned vertically with respect to the table's element box using the property `vertical-align`. In this case, only the values `top`, `middle`, and `bottom` will be honored. Any other `vertical-align` value set on a caption will be treated as `top`.

right

Places the caption's element box to the right of the table box. Otherwise, this has the same effect as the value `left`.

Notes

If the value of `caption-side` is `right` or `left`, the caption will be placed outside the table's element box, including any margins. Since setting the `width` of a left- or right-side caption to `auto` leaves the actual width up to the user agent, it is recommended that authors set explicit widths for such captions.

Examples

```
caption {caption-side: left; width: 10em; text-align: right;
    vertical-align: top;}
td.label {display: table-caption; caption-side: bottom;
    margin-top: 0.33em; width: 80%;}
table {caption-side: top;}
```

Related Properties

`display`

clear

`clear` prevents an element from being displayed next to floated elements.

Summary

Value Syntax

none | left | right | both | inherit

Initial Value

Percentages
n/a

Inherited
no

Applies to
block-level elements

Media Groups
visual

4

Values

none
Floated elements may appear on either side of the element.

left
Floated elements may not appear to the left of the element. If a floated element would appear to the left of the element, the top margin of the element is increased until the top outer edge of the element's border is just below the bottom outer edge of the floated element.

right
Floated elements may not appear to the right of the element. The top margin will be increased as necessary to ensure this.

both
Floated elements may not appear on either side of the element, and the top margin is increased, if necessary, to ensure this.

Notes

The value for `clear` only affects the display of an element with regard to floated elements which appear earlier in the document. If an element has descendant elements which are floated, they are not considered for the purposes of `clear` on that element.

Examples

```
h2 {clear: right;}
img.illus {float: left; clear: left;}
```

Related Properties

```
float
```

clip

clip defines the area outside which an absolutely positioned element's content is not visible.

Summary

Value Syntax
<shape> | auto | inherit

Initial Value
auto

Percentages
n/a

Inherited
no

Applies to
block-level and replaced elements

Media Groups
visual

Values

<shape>
A shape descriptor. As of CSS2, there is only one valid shape: rect(top right bottom left). According to CSS2, the four values within rect(...) define offsets from the content edge of the positioned element, and each one may be either a length value or auto. Thus, rect(10px 10px 10px 10px) would describe a clipping region inset by ten pixels from each edge of the content area. However, Internet Explorer implemented this shape as rect(top-x top-y width height). Thus, rect(10px 10px 20px 10px) would define a clip rectangle which begins 10 pixels below the top of the content area, and 10 pixels to the right of the left edge, and which is 20 pixels wide by 10 pixels tall. Furthermore, Explorer treats clip as a method of clipping all aspects of an element—background, borders, content, and anything else.

auto
The clipping region is equivalent to the content area of the positioned element.

Notes

The value given for `clip` applies only if the property `overflow` has been set to a value other than `visible` for the affected element.

As of this writing, the specification and implementation were still out of step with regard to the syntax of `rect(...)`. There were proposals to change the meaning of `clip` to match Internet Explorer, and also to reintroduce the original meaning of `clip` as another property, but this had not occurred by the time this text went to press.

In either case, it is possible to define clipping regions which are larger than the element's content area. This will not affect the layout of the content, but may affect how much of it is visible. For example, imagine an element which is seven lines tall, but which contains seventeen lines of text. If the `overflow` is set to `hidden` and the clipping region is set to `clip: auto`, then only the first seven lines of content will be visible; the rest will be hidden. Now assume a clipping region of `rect(0 0 -1em 0)`, using the W3C syntax instead of the Explorer method. This will extend the bottom of the clipping area down by one em—effectively, the height of a line—and so the eighth line will be visible. This will not change the size of the element's box, however, so it is possible that the eighth line will be drawn outside the borders of the element, or within its padding, or possibly overlapping the border. This would also be possible in Internet Explorer, although with a different syntax: something like `rect(0 0 200px 8em)`, assuming that the element's box is known to be 200 pixels wide and `7em` tall.

Examples

```
div.aside {position: absolute; width: 50%; height: auto;
   overflow: hidden; clip: rect(1em 0.5em 1em 0.5em);}
p.scroller {height: 7em; overflow: scroll; clip: auto;}
#spillout {position: absolute; overflow: hidden;
   clip: rect(0 0 -5em 0);}
```

Related Properties

`overflow`

color

`color` sets the foreground color of an element (typically, the color of the text).

Summary

Value Syntax
<color> | inherit

Initial Value
UA dependent

Percentages
n/a

Inherited
yes

Applies to
all elements

Media Groups
visual

Values

<color>
Any permitted color value.

Notes

It is strongly recommended that authors who set a foreground color
on an element also set a background color for the same element.
Omitting the background leads to the possibility of color conflicts
among the author's styles, reader stylesheets, and the user agent's
defaults. For example, if an author sets an H1 with a class of title
to have a white foreground, and a reader's stylesheet sets the
background color of all H1 elements to be white, then the combination
of the two could lead to an H1 with white text on a white background.

The value declared for color is used as the default color of any
borders which may appear on the element. This default can be
overridden with the various border-color-related properties.

Using the keyword inherit with the property color will result
in a sickly green in Navigator 4.x.

Examples

```
h1 {color: maroon;}
p.sunny {color: yellow;}
a:link {color: blue;}
a:visited {color: purple;}
```

Related Properties
border-color

content

content defines content to be inserted in generated content
operations.

Summary

Value Syntax
[<string> | <uri> | <counter> | attr(X) | open-quote |
close-quote | no-open-quote | no-close-quote]+
| inherit

Initial Value
empty string (" ")

Percentages
n/a

Inherited
no

Applies to
:before and :after pseudo-elements

Media Groups
all

Values

<string>
Any permitted string value. This is always enclosed in
quotation marks.

<uri>
A pointer to an external resource such as an image. If the user agent
cannot display the resource, then the reference is ignored. It is
theoretically possible to include the contents of an entire text or
HTML file in this manner. If a resource such as an image is included
in the document, there is no way to provide an alternate text
description or other accessibility features for the resource.

<counter>

There are two possible forms of this value: `counter(name, style?)` and `counters(name, string,? style?)`. In both cases, the content will be the value of the named counter at that point in the document, rendered in the optional style value (`decimal` by default). In the case of `counters(...)`, the optional string value indicates a string to follow each instance of the named counter. See `counter-increment` for more details.

attr(X)

Causes the insertion of the value of attribute X for the selector's subject. For example, it is possible to display the value of the `alt` attribute of an image using this value. If the attribute does not exist for that element, an empty string is returned.

open-quote

Causes the insertion of the appropriate string specified using the property `quotes`.

close-quote

Causes the insertion of the appropriate string specified using the property `quotes`.

no-open-quote

Prevents the insertion of the appropriate string specified using the property `quotes`. However, the nesting level of the quotation marks is still increased.

no-close-quote

Prevents the insertion of the appropriate string specified using the property `quotes`. However, the nesting level of the quotation marks is still decreased.

Notes

Any styles which are applied to the parent element will be applied to the generated content. It is also possible to style the generated content separately from the contents of its parent.

Examples

```
p.aside:before {content: "aside - "; font-weight: bold;
   color: gray;}
p:after {content: url(paramark.gif);}
li:before {content: counters(list-count, ".", lower-roman);}
a:after {content: "[" attr(href) "]"; font-size: smaller;}
```

Related Properties
:after, :before, counter-increment, counter-reset, quotes

counter-increment

counter-increment increases the value of a named counter.

Summary

Value Syntax
[<name> <integer>?]+ | none | inherit

Initial Value
none

Percentages
n/a

Inherited
no

Applies to
all elements

Media Groups
all

Values

<name>
The name of a counter. The name can be any string value.
If the name has not been previously reset using the property
counter-reset for the particular scope in which it occurs (see
the notes section), the named counter is assumed to have been
set to zero by the root element of the document.

<integer>
Defines an increment for the named counter each time the
element appears in the document. This increment can be zero,
or even negative. If no integer is provided, the counter is
incremented by one.

none
No increment is performed.

Notes

If an element is set to display: none, then any counters for
that element will *not* be incremented. If the element is set to

`visibility`: `hidden`, on the other hand, then any counters will be incremented. If an element has both `counter-increment` and `counter-reset` declared, then the counter is first reset and then incremented. More than one counter may be reset at a time.

Although counters may be incremented (and reset) on a given element, the property `content` is what causes the counter to be displayed. It does this with its two counter-related values, `counter(name, style?)` and `counters(name, string?, style?)`. These are explained here due to their dependence on `counter-increment` to operate effectively.

`counter(name, style)` is used to increment a counter within its current scope. The `style` portion is optional, and may use any of the permitted values for `list-style-type`, including `circle`, `disc`, and `square`. Every time an element resets a named counter using the property `counter-reset`, it creates a scope for that counter. Different scopes can use the same named counter without collision; thus, the counting of labels for nested lists can be easily represented. For example, the traditional HTML method of counting nested lists can be represented as:

```
ol {counter-reset: list-count;}
li:before {content: counter(list-count) ". ";
    counter-increment: list-count;}
```

As ordered lists are nested deeper, each "level" creates its own scoped version of `list-count`. Since the default list style is `decimal`, it does not need to be specified here.

Use of the value `counters(name, string, style)` results in an accumulation of scoped counters, instead of just displaying the counter for the current scope. Thus, changing the previous example to use `counters(list-count, ".")` would result in counters in the style "1.2", "1.2.1", and so on. At each nesting level, the newly scoped counter and the string will be added on to the previous counter(s). Similarly, `counters(list-count, "-")` would result in "1-2", "1-2-1", and so on.

Examples

```
h2:before {color: green; counter-increment: section;
    content: "Section " counter(section, upper-alpha) ". ";}
ol li:before {counter-increment: list-count;
```

```
  content: counters(item, ".", decimal; font-style:
  italic;}
ol.thirds li {counter-increment: triples 3 list-count 1;}
```

Related Properties
content, counter-reset

counter-reset

counter-reset sets a named counter to a specific value.

Summary

Value Syntax
[<name> <integer>?]+ | none | inherit

Initial Value
none

Percentages
n/a

Inherited
no

Applies to
all elements

Media Groups
all

Values

<name>
The named counter to be reset.

<integer>
The number to which the named counter should be reset. If no
integer is given, then the counter is reset to 0. Negative values
are permitted.

none
No reset is performed.

Notes

If an element has both `counter-increment` and `counter-reset` declared, then the counter is first reset and then incremented. More than one counter may be reset at a time.

Examples

```
h1 {counter-reset: chapter section sub-section;}
pre.example {counter-reset: examples;}
ol.fifth {counter-reset: list-counter -5;}
```

Related Properties

`content, counter-increment`

cursor

`cursor` changes the appearance of the cursor (mouse pointer) when it is hovering over an element; that is, at the time when the pointer is within the element's box.

Summary

Value Syntax
```
[ [<uri> ,]* [ auto | crosshair | default | pointer |
move | e-resize | ne-resize | nw-resize | n-resize |
se-resize | sw-resize | s-resize | w-resize| text |
wait | help ] ] | inherit
```

Initial Value
`auto`

Percentages
n/a

Inherited
yes

Applies to
all elements

Media Groups
visual, interactive

Values

<uri>
A pointer to a resource containing a cursor appearance. If the user agent cannot resolve the URL, or cannot handle the resource to which it points, then it must use a generic cursor. Since there is no standard for cursor resources in CSS, this feature is functionally disabled in all browsers known at the time of this writing.

auto
The user agent determines the cursor appearance for a given context.

crosshair
A crosshair symbol not unlike the plus sign (+).

default
The user-agent or platform-dependent default cursor. Usually an arrow, but may be something else due to the operating system, user-installed software, or other factors.

pointer
The cursor which is used to indicate that a link is being hovered. On most systems, this is a small hand with a pointing finger.

move
The cursor gives the appearance that the element can be moved. On many systems, this is a pair of two-way arrows in a cross formation, not unlike taking the crosshair cursor and adding arrowheads to the four points.

e-resize
The cursor gives the appearance of allowing size to be increased to the right. This is usually an arrow pointing to the right.

ne-resize
The cursor gives the appearance of allowing size to be increased both to the right and upward. This is usually an arrow pointing in the direction of the top right corner of the display.

nw-resize
The cursor gives the appearance of allowing size to be increased both to the left and upward. This is usually an arrow pointing in the direction of the top left corner of the display.

n-resize

The cursor gives the appearance of allowing size to be increased upward. This is usually an arrow pointing to the top of the display.

se-resize

The cursor gives the appearance of allowing size to be increased both downward and to the right. This is usually an arrow pointing in the direction of the bottom right corner of the display.

sw-resize

The cursor gives the appearance of allowing size to be increased both downward and to the right. This is usually an arrow pointing in the direction of the bottom left corner of the display.

s-resize

The cursor gives the appearance of allowing size to be increased downward. This is usually an arrow pointing to the bottom of the display.

w-resize

The cursor gives the appearance of allowing size to be increased to the left. This is usually an arrow pointing to the left.

text

The cursor gives the appearance of allowing a text selection, as with drag-selection of text to be copied. This is usually an "I-bar," so named for its resemblance to a capital "I."

wait

The cursor gives the appearance that the program is busy and that the user should wait. This is typically an hourglass or watch icon.

help

The cursor gives the appearance that there is help available. This is typically rendered as a question mark.

Notes

Because users are generally very attuned to changes in the cursor's appearance and expect that certain cursors have certain meanings, authors should use caution in employing this property.

Examples

```
p {cursor: text;}
div.confuse {cursor: wait;}
a.helpsys:link, a.helpsys:visited {cursor: help;}
```

Related Properties
None

direction

`direction` indicates the writing direction to be used in the rendering of an element.

Summary

Value Syntax
`ltr | rtl | inherit`

Initial Value
`ltr`

Percentages
n/a

Inherited
yes

Applies to
all elements, but see notes

Media Groups
visual

Values

ltr
The text is written left-to-right.

rtl
The text is written right-to-left.

Notes

`direction` will affect not only the writing direction of text, but also the order in which table columns are laid out and the direction in which content will horizontally overflow an element's content area. It also determines the placement of a partial line at the end of an element which has been set to `text-align: justify`.

Although `direction` can be applied to any element, it will have an effect on inline elements only if the property `unicode-bidi` is set to `embed` or `bidi-override`.

Examples

```
*:lang(en) {direction: ltr;}
p.hebrew {direction: rtl;}
```

Related Properties

`unicode-bidi`

display

`display` affects the most basic presentation of an element,
effectively classing the element as a certain type of element.
The rendering of the element may depend heavily on its display
type, and certain properties will only work on elements that have
specific `display` values.

Summary

Value Syntax

inline | block | list-item | run-in | compact | marker |
table | inline-table | table-row-group | table-header-group |
table-footer-group | table-row | table-column-group |
table-column | table-cell | table-caption | none | inherit

Initial Value

inline

Percentages

n/a

Inherited

no

Applies to

all elements

Media Groups

all

Values

inline

This value causes an element to generate an inline-level box; for
example, the HTML elements STRONG, CODE, or EM (among others).
The element will generate one or more inline boxes when it
is displayed.

block

This value causes an element to generate a block-level box; for example, the HTML elements P, H1, or PRE (among others). The element will generate a block box when it is displayed.

list-item

This value causes an element to generate both a block box and a list-item inline box. Under HTML, the LI element is the only example of such an element.

run-in

Under certain conditions, this value will cause the element to be "inserted" into the beginning of the following element. If an element A is set to display: run-in and is followed by a block-level element B, then A becomes the first inline-level box of B. If the element following A is not block-level, then A becomes a block-level box.

compact

Under certain conditions, this value will cause the element to be placed to one side of the following element. If an element A is set to display: compact and is followed by a block-level element B, and B is neither floated nor absolutely positioned, then A is formatted as a single-line inline box. If A cannot be formatted as a single line, it becomes a block-level box. If A can be formatted in a single line, its width is compared to the width of the margin to one side of B; the margin chosen (right or left) is determined by the value of the property direction for element B. If the width of A is less than the width of the chosen margin, then it is placed within that margin, with the baseline of element A aligned with the baseline in the first line of element B. The height of A will affect the height of the first line in element B. If A cannot fit into the chosen margin, then A becomes a block-level box.

marker

This value will set generated content to be a marker; thus, it should be used only in conjunction with the :before and :after pseudo-elements when they are set on block-level elements. In all other cases, marker is treated as inline. Markers are placed in the margin of the associated element, but can overlap the content of the element with which they are associated. Thus, authors should set a width on the marker box, and also set the left or right margin of the element such that it will be wide enough to contain the marker without overlap. If the marker's width is set to auto, then its width is that of its content. If the width of the marker is too small to display all of the content, the overflow of the content is controlled by the value for `overflow`. The height of a marker box is set using the property `line-height`, *not* `height`. The distance between the marker and the main element (which is known as the *principal box*) is controlled by the property `marker-offset`. For markers placed before the principal box, the baseline of the marker is vertically aligned with the baseline of the first line in the principal box. Similarly, for markers placed after the principal box, the baselines of the marker and the last line in the principal box are vertically aligned. If the principal box does not contain any text, then the bottom outer edge of the trailing marker is aligned with the bottom edge of the principal box's bottom outer edge. Finally, a marker box will be created only if the value of the property `content` actually generates any content to be displayed.

table
This value causes an element to generate a block-level table box. This is analogous to the HTML element `TABLE`.

inline-table
This value causes an element to generate an inline-level table box. While there is no analogue in HTML, it can be envisioned as a traditional HTML table which can appear in the middle of a line of text.

table-cell
This value declares the element to be a table cell. This is analogous to the HTML element `TD`.

table-row
This value declares the element to be a row of table cells. This is analogous to the HTML element `TR`.

table-row-group
This value declares the element to be a group of table rows. This is analogous to the HTML element `TBODY`.

table-column
This value declares the element to be a column of table cells. This is analogous to the HTML element `COL`.

table-column-group
This value declares the element to be a group of table columns. This is analogous to the HTML element `COLGROUP`.

table-header-group
This value declares the element to be a group of cells which is always visible at the top of the table, placed before any row or row-groups but after any top-aligned table captions. In paged media, the user agent may place the contents of this element at the top of each page which the table spans. This is analogous to the HTML element THEAD.

table-footer-group
This value declares the element to be a group of cells which is always visible at the bottom of the table, placed after any row or row-groups but before any bottom-aligned table captions. In paged media, the user agent may place the contents of this element at the bottom of each page which the table spans. This is analogous to the HTML element TFOOT.

table-caption
This value declares the element to be a caption for a table. This is analogous to the HTML element CAPTION.

none
The element will generate no boxes at all, and thus will neither be displayed nor impact the layout of the document. Any descendant elements will also be prevented from appearing, regardless of the value of display for those elements.

Notes
The default value of inline is new to CSS2. Under CSS1, the default value was block, but this made a lot of people very angry and was widely regarded as a bad move.

display can be used to affect aural rendering of a document; see the entry on speak in Chapter 6 for more details.

Authors are urged to use extreme caution when using display in a document language which already has a strong display hierarchy, such as HTML. Considerable havoc could result from setting all elements to be block, for example; declaring everything to be inline could be just as bad. On the other hand, in a language like XML which has no predefined display semantics, use of display is a matter of necessity.

Examples
```
img.illus {display: block;}
li {display: list-item;}
```

```
h3 {display: run-in;}
* {display: inline;}
```

Related Properties
visibility

empty-cells

empty-cells is used in the separate-border table layout model to control the rendering of table cells which have no visible content.

Summary

Value Syntax
show | hide | inherit

Initial Value
show

Percentages
n/a

Inherited
yes

Applies to
elements with a display of table-cell

Media Groups
visual

Values

show
The borders of an empty cell are rendered.

hide
The borders of an empty cell are not drawn.

Notes

A cell is considered to be *empty* if it has no visible content. This can apply to cells which are devoid of content, cells which contain content that has been made invisible with the property `visibility`, and elements which have been suppressed with the use of the property `display`. Visible content is any content which is drawn within the cell, the non-breaking space entity (` `), and any other whitespace besides the carriage-return, linefeed, tab, and space characters (ASCII codes `\0D`, `\0A`, `\09`, and `\20`, respectively).

`empty-cells` will be honored only when the property `border-collapse` is set to `separate`. If `border-collapse` is set to `collapse`, then `empty-cells` (and any associated values) will be ignored.

Examples

```
table.wide {border-collapse: separate; empty-cells: show;}
td.blank {empty-cells: hide;}
```

Related Properties

`border-collapse`

float

`float` causes an element to be moved to one side of the parent element's content area, which allows other content to flow around it.

Summary

Value Syntax
`left | right | none | inherit`

Initial Value
`none`

Percentages
n/a

Inherited
no

Applies to
all but positioned elements and generated content

Media Groups
visual

Values

left
The element is floated to the left side of its parent element's content area. Following content will flow around the floated element to the right.

right
The element is floated to the right side of its parent element's content area. Following content will flow around the floated element to the left.

none
The element is not floated.

Notes

For the rules which govern floating behavior, please see Chapter 1. Under CSS2, positioned elements and generated content cannot be floated.

An image which has been floated will retain its intrinsic width. Text elements, however, should have a value assigned for `width`; otherwise, results can be unpredictable. According to the CSS2 specification, the width of floated text elements will tend toward zero unless some explicit width has been assigned. Thus, a floated text element with no assigned width could be as narrow as a single character wide, or perhaps the width of the longest word within the element. Since there is no precisely defined behavior in such a case, each user agent will likely differ from every other user agent. In order to avoid uncertainty, authors should be careful to ensure that floated text elements have a declared width.

In effect, floating an element causes it to reset its `display` to `block`, regardless of its original display level. The only exception is if the original `display` was `none`, in which case the element will still not be rendered, and `float` will have no effect.

While the content of following elements flows around the floated element, the element boxes of those following elements will stretch under the floated element. In other words, while the foreground is reflowed to avoid overwriting the float, the background will "slide under" the float. This is necessary to avoid non-rectangular backgrounds, in the case of an element whose top is at the middle of a float, but whose height is such that some of its content flows beneath the float. The unwelcome side effect is that any element which is completely next to a float, and which also has a visible background, will have its background drawn under the float. This is also true of any borders which are set on elements next to floats. If authors wish to ensure that visible backgrounds and borders are not drawn under floats, they should be sure to set the property `clear` to move said elements below any floated element.

Support for `float` exists in all CSS-aware browsers, but unfortunately it is also the property most plagued by bugs. Floating text elements is one sore point, and so is floating elements within other floated elements, as well as floating within tables. Authors are urged to undertake extra browser testing when using `float`.

Examples
```
img.figure {float: right;}
p.aside {float: left; width: 25%;}
```

Related Properties
`clear, width`

font

`font` is a shorthand property used to affect the rendering of text.

Summary

Value Syntax
```
[ [ <font-style> || <font-variant> || <font-weight> ]?
<font-size> [ / <line-height> ]? <font-family> ] | caption |
icon | menu | message-box | small-caption | status-bar |
inherit
```

Initial Value
not defined for shorthand properties

Percentages
allowed on `<font-size>` and `<line-height>`; refer to `font-size` of parent element

Inherited
yes

Applies to
all elements

Media Groups
visual

Values

<font-style>
Any permitted value for the property `font-style` (see `font-style` for more details).

<font-variant>
Any permitted value for the property `font-variant` (see `font-variant` for more details).

<font-weight>
Any permitted value for the property `font-weight` (see `font-weight` for more details).

<font-size>
Any permitted value for the property `font-size` (see `font-size` for more details).

<line-height>
Any permitted value for the property `line-height` (see `line-height` for more details).

<font-family>
Any permitted value for the property `font-family` (see `font-family` for more details).

caption
The font used by the operating system for captioned controls (e.g., buttons and drop-down menus). This is one of the "system font" values.

icon
The font used by the operating system to label icons. This is one of the "system font" values.

menu
The font used by the operating system in menus (e.g., drop-down menus and menu lists). This is one of the "system font" values.

message-box
The font used by the operating system within dialog boxes (e.g., warning dialogs). This is one of the "system font" values.

small-caption
The font used by the operating system to label small controls. This is one of the "system font" values.

status-bar
The font used by the operating system in window status bars. This is one of the "system font" values.

Notes
System font keywords must be declared alone. If the author wishes to change the appearance of the element's text when employing a system font, this must be done with the more specific font properties (e.g., font-size).

If the author does use a system font keyword, then the bare minimum value for font is the <font-size> and <font-family> keywords. All font values which do not involve system fonts and do not include a <line-height> keyword must end with the <font-size> and <font-family> keywords, in that order.

Any keyword values which are not given in the font declaration cause the corresponding properties to be reset to their default values. Thus, if the keyword <font-style> is omitted, then the property font-style is set to its default value, normal. The properties font-size-adjust and font-stretch cannot be provided in a font declaration, and must be declared separately. However, use of the property font will still reset the values of font-size-adjust and font-stretch to their defaults.

The "system font" values are not well supported as of this writing, but this is expected to change rapidly. One area to watch is support for line-height (see the entry later in this chapter for more details).

Examples
```
h1 {font: bold italic small-caps 250%/1.2 sans-serif;}
pre {font: 1em Courier, "Courier New", Mishawka, monospace;}
div.footer {font: italic smaller/0.8em Times, TimesNR, serif;}
div.dialog {font: message-box;}
```

Related Properties

font-family, font-size, font-style, font-variant, font-weight, line-height

font-family

font-family allows the author to provide a comma-separated list of specific font families, plus a generic type of font family, to be used in the rendering of an element's text.

Summary

Value Syntax
[[<family-name> | <generic-family>],]*
[<family-name> | <generic-family>] | inherit

Initial Value
UA dependent

Percentages
n/a

Inherited
yes

Applies to
all elements

Media Groups
visual

Values

<family-name>
The name of a specific font (e.g., Times, Helvetica, or Arial). Font names which contain whitespace should be quoted, using either single- or double-quotation marks. If the font name is not quoted, then any sequence of whitespace characters within the font name will be converted to a single space, and any leading or trailing whitespace in the font name will be ignored. Technically, font names which do not contain whitespace can be quoted, but this is not recommended, as it can confuse some user agents.

<generic-family>
One of five defined generic font family keywords: serif, sans-serif, monospace, cursive, and fantasy. The

generic-family keywords cannot be quoted. The user agent must maintain a list of specific fonts for each generic family, and will select a font for use from among that list. Of the five generic-family keywords, two are problematic: `cursive` and `fantasy`. Because most cursive fonts render fairly badly on computer monitors, many systems do not have any cursive fonts available. Even if a cursive font is available, it will generally make the document's legibility very poor, so caution should be used in the employment of cursive fonts. On the other side of the coin, `fantasy` tends to mean "any font which does not fit into the other four generic families." The potentially infinite variability of fantasy fonts—some may be "symbol" or "dingbat" fonts, while others may represent invented languages such as Klingon, and still others may simply be too "arty" to read—means that no two systems are likely to map `fantasy` to the same font. (This problem exists, to a lesser degree, with cursive fonts, which tend to be very different from one another.) These factors make `fantasy` almost unusable in the real world, and extreme caution should be exercised in its use.

Notes

See Chapter 1 for more details on font selection in CSS.

When rendering an element's text, the user agent will attempt to use the fonts in the order in which they are provided. Thus, given the value `Times, Adams, serif`, a user agent will first attempt to use Times. If Times is not available, or if it does not contain the needed character, then the user agent will attempt to use Adams. If Adams is either unsuitable or unavailable, then the user agent will go to the last entry on the list, which directs it to use any available serif font. If the generic family has been omitted from the value, then the user agent would have been forced to use its default font (generally set by the user in a preferences dialog). Note that specific fonts do not have to fall into the same generic family. It is perfectly legal to specify Times, Helvetica, Courier, and "Minion Web" in the same `font-family` value.

Because of the possibility that a given user agent will not have the specific fonts requested, authors are strongly encouraged to provide a last-ditch fallback in the form of a generic-family keyword at the end of every `font-family` value.

It is possible to place generic-family keywords at any point in a `font-family` value. However, since the presence of a generic-family keyword will often lead to the selection of *some* available font, any specific fonts listed after a generic-family keyword will likely never be chosen. It can be useful to provide multiple generic-family keywords at the end of a `font-family` value, especially if the preferred generic family is an uncommon type such as `cursive`.

Examples

```
h1 {font-family: Helvetica, Arial, Verdana, sans-serif;}
pre {font-family: monospace;}
p {font-family: Times, "Times New Roman", TimesNR,
    "New Century Schoolbook", serif;}
div.signature {font-family: "Meyer Light", cursive, serif;}
```

Related Properties
`font`

font-size

`font-size` affects the size of an element's text.

Summary

Value Syntax
xx-small | x-small | small | medium | large | x-large | xx-large | larger | smaller | <length> | <percentage> | inherit

Initial Value
medium

Percentages
refer to parent element's font size

Inherited
yes

Applies to
all elements

Media Groups
visual

Values

xx-small
Sets the element's text to be a size smaller than that which results from the value `x-small`. The exact size is not defined by CSS.

x-small
Sets the element's text to be a size smaller than that which results from the value `small`. The exact size is not defined by CSS.

small
Sets the element's text to be a size smaller than that which results from the value `medium`. The exact size is not defined by CSS.

medium
Sets the element's text to be a size smaller than that which results from the value `large`, and larger than that which results from the value `small`. The exact size is not defined by CSS.

large
Sets the element's text to be a size larger than that which results from the value `medium`. The exact size is not defined by CSS, although `medium` text should be equivalent to the user's default setting (for example, the size of unstyled paragraph text).

x-large
Sets the element's text to be a size larger than that which results from the value `large`. The exact size is not defined by CSS.

xx-large
Sets the element's text to be a size larger than that which results from the value `x-large`. The exact size is not defined by CSS.

larger
Sets the element's text to be larger than that of its parent. This is accomplished by using the absolute-size scaling factor (see notes) to increase the size of the text.

smaller
Sets the element's text to be smaller than that of its parent. This is accomplished by using the absolute-size scaling factor (see notes) to decrease the size of the text.

<length>
Any permitted length value. Negative length values are not permitted for `font-size`.

<percentage>
Sets the element's text size relative to that of its parent. For example, `font-size: 50%` will make the element's text half the size of its parent element's text. The resulting value of `font-size` for a percentage calculation is actually the computed font-size which results from the calculation. Thus, if an element's font is set to

a percentage and is calculated to be seven pixels tall, then its font-size is set to 7px, and it is this value which is inherited by any descendant elements.

Notes

In order to increase the robustness and scalability of styles, authors are encouraged to use percentages and em lengths in their stylesheets. Since these values will set font-size in relation to the default font size (or other elements), they are vastly preferable to absolute-length units such as points. Furthermore, setting common elements (such as BODY or P) to a font-size less than 1em (or 100%) is discouraged, as this will make most text smaller than the user's default setting. In many cases, this will make the text too small for comfortable reading.

The computed font-size values of the absolute-size keywords xx-small through xx-large are not precisely defined, but they do have a known relationship to one another. These values relate to one another via a scaling factor internal to the user agent. CSS1 suggested a factor of 1.5, but CSS2 changed this to 1.2; however, user agents are not required to use any particular scaling factor. In fact, different fonts may have different scaling factors.

In any case, adjacent keywords in the progression will have the same size relationship. This relationship is controlled by the scaling factor. For example, assume that medium is equivalent to 10pt. Given a scaling factor of 1.2, then large would be equivalent to 12pt, x-large to 14.4pt (12 times 1.2), and so on. Similarly, small would be equivalent to 8.33pt (10 divided by 1.2), x-small to 6.94pt, and so on.

While user agents might be expected to recompute the actual sizes of these keywords if the user changes the default font size, in practice most do not. Instead, they assign unchanging font sizes to the absolute-size keywords.

Despite what one might expect, providing a length value for font-size may not guarantee the actual size of the font. This can occur for a number of reasons.

First, the value of font-size is actually setting the height of the character box for each character which is displayed, not the height of the character glyph itself. Since font character glyphs are rarely exactly the same height as their character boxes, the actual measured size of the character glyph may not precisely match the value given for `font-size`. In most cases, the actual height of the characters will be less than the `font-size` value, but in some cases they may be taller.

If the preferred font is not available, and a value has been given for the property `font-size-adjust`, then the actual font-size of the font used may be different than that which the author has specified.

In addition, the user agent may maintain bounds past which it will not allow the computed value of `font-size` to go. In most cases, this will be to prevent fonts from becoming too small to read, but upper `font-size` bounds may also be enforced.

Finally, user agents may provide the user with the ability to alter font sizes, regardless of how the author sets them. These range from user stylesheets to interface features like "Text Zoom" in Internet Explorer 5 for the Macintosh, or the "Page Zoom" found in Opera.

Examples
```
h1 {font-size: 225%;}
div.legal {font-size: 0.75em;}
```

Related Properties
`font`, `font-size-adjust`

font-size-adjust

`font-size-adjust` can be used to improve the legibility of alternate font choices.

Summary

Value Syntax
`<number> | none | inherit`

Initial Value
none

Percentages
n/a

Inherited
yes

Applies to
all elements

Media Groups
visual

Values

<number>
The aspect value of the first font listed in the value of the property
font-family. This value is used in the equation *fs x (fa/aa) = as*,
where *fs* is the declared value of font-size for the element, *fa* is
the declared value of font-size-adjust, *aa* is the aspect value
of the actual font to be used, and *as* is the computed font-size
for the element.

none
No size adjustments should be made to alternate font choices.

Notes

Although font-size-adjust cannot be set as a keyword of the
property font, its value will be reset to none for an element if
font is also declared for that element. Thus, any element which
uses both font and font-size-adjust must have the properties
in that order: font first, and font-size-adjust second.

In order to understand font-size-adjust a little better, let us
consider a hypothetical example. Suppose that an author declares
that an element should use (in order of preference) the fonts "Kathryn
Light" and "Meyer Web." The aspect value of Kathryn Light, which
is the ratio of the x-height to the height of its character box, is 0.42.
Knowing this, the page author sets font-size-adjust to 0.42
and also declares the element's font-size to be 18px.

A user views the page with a system that does not have Kathryn
Light, but does have Meyer Web. The aspect value for Meyer Web
is 0.42. The user agent then performs the following calculation:
18px times (0.42/0.23) = 32.87px. This will be the font-size
used to display the element using Meyer Web. Although this may
seem like an enormous difference, the legibility of the element's
text will be approximately the same as if it had used the first-choice
font. Without this size adjustment, the element's text would be
very difficult to read using Meyer Web.

In practice, this property is rarely used and even less often supported.

Examples

```
p.sig {font: 125% Author, Braggadaccio, cursive;
   font-size-adjust: 0.33;}
h1 {font-family: Verdana, sans-serif; font-size-adjust:
0.58;}
```

Related Properties

```
font, font-size
```

font-stretch

font-stretch makes text characters wider or narrower than the font's default character width.

Summary

Value Syntax
```
normal | wider | narrower | ultra-condensed |
extra-condensed | condensed | semi-condensed | semi-expanded |
expanded | extra-expanded | ultra-expanded | inherit
```

Initial Value
```
normal
```

Percentages
n/a

Inherited
yes

Applies to
all elements

Media Groups
visual

Values

ultra-condensed
The text characters in the element will be narrowed extremely, rendering them narrower than if the value were extra-condensed. CSS does not specify how this is accomplished, nor does it point out the mechanism for calculating the final character width.

extra-condensed
The text characters in the element will be narrowed significantly, making them narrower than if the value were condensed. CSS

does not specify how this is accomplished, nor does it reveal the mechanism for calculating the final character width.

condensed

The text characters in the element will be narrowed, more so than if the value were `semi-condensed`. CSS does not specify how this is accomplished, nor does it disclose the mechanism for calculating the final character width.

semi-condensed

The text characters in the element will be slightly narrowed, making them narrower than if the value were `normal`. CSS does not specify how this is accomplished, nor does it explain the mechanism by which the final character width is calculated.

normal

The text characters in the element are of normal width.

semi-expanded

The text characters in the element will be slightly widened, making them wider than if the value were `normal`. CSS does not specify how this is accomplished, nor does it show the mechanism for calculating the final character width.

expanded

The text characters in the element will be widened, making them wider than if the value were `semi-expanded`. CSS does not specify how this is accomplished, nor does it present the mechanism for calculating the final character width.

extra-expanded

The text characters in the element will be widened greatly, making them wider than if the value were `expanded`. CSS does not specify how this is accomplished, nor does it explain the mechanism for calculating the final character width.

ultra-expanded

The text characters in the element will be widened extremely, making them wider than if the value were `extra-expanded`. CSS does not specify how this is accomplished, nor does it divulge the mechanism for calculating the final character width.

wider

The width of text characters in the element will be wider than those of their parent element. In effect, this moves the `font-stretch` value up one notch in the list of keywords above, so that if the parent element's `font-stretch` is `semi-expanded`, then the element's value will be `expanded`. The value cannot be increased past `ultra-expanded`.

narrower
The width of text characters in the element will be narrower than those of their parent element. In effect, this moves the `font-stretch` value down one notch in the list of keywords above, so that if the parent element's `font-stretch` is `normal`, then the element's value will be `semi-condensed`. The value cannot be increased past `ultra-condensed`.

Notes
Although `font-stretch` cannot be set as a keyword of the property `font`, its value will be reset to `none` for an element if `font` is also declared for that element. Thus, any element which uses both `font` and `font-stretch` must have the properties in that order: `font` first, and `font-stretch` second.

In practice, this property is rarely used and even less often supported.

Examples
```
em {font-stretch: extra-expanded;}
div.narrow {font-stretch: ultra-condensed;}
p {font-stretch: normal;}
```

Related Properties
`font`

font-style

`font-style` determines the use of one of three font faces to be used in the rendering of a given element's text.

Summary

Value Syntax
`normal | italic | oblique | inherit`

Initial Value
`normal`

Percentages
n/a

Inherited
yes

Applies to
all elements

Media Groups
visual

Values

normal
Specifies a normal font face; that is, whatever is the default face for the font in use. In most fonts, this results in an upright font.

italic
Specifies an italic font face; that is, one which is slanted and in which the characters have been modified to improve legibility in their slanted state. These are often referred to as Cursive or Italic faces. If no italic font face is available, the user agent may select one which is labeled "oblique."

oblique
Specifies an oblique font face; that is, one which is slanted. These are often referred to as Oblique or Incline faces. In many cases, an oblique face is simply a normal face which has been computationally slanted.

Notes
As of this writing, there is no visual difference between the values italic and oblique in Web browsers. This makes the value oblique fairly unnecessary, but in the future better support in Web browsers may bring oblique back into common usage.

Examples
```
p.slant {font-style: oblique;}
blockquote {font-style: italic;}
blockquote em {font-style: normal;}
```

Related Properties
font

font-variant

`font-variant` determines the use of one of two font faces to be used in the rendering of a given element's text.

Summary

Value Syntax
`normal | small-caps | inherit`

Initial Value
`normal`

Percentages
n/a

Inherited
yes

Applies to
all elements

Media Groups
visual

Values

normal
Specifies a normal font face; that is, whatever is the default face for the font in use. In the context of this property, this value effectively means that the font should not be small-caps.

small-caps
Specifies a small-caps face; that is, a face in which lowercase characters are rendered as capital letters which are smaller than the letters used for uppercase characters. If no such face is available, the user agent may simulate one by computationally scaling capital letters to get the desired effect.

Notes

Since lowercase characters in a small-caps font are rendered as capital letters of reduced size, they may suffer from reduced legibility as well. For example, a small-caps font in which the uppercase characters are 12 pixels tall (due to the rule `font-size: 12px`, perhaps) may use 10-pixel-tall capitals for lowercase characters.

Under CSS2, user agents are allowed to simulate the small-caps effect by rendering all text in capital letters of the same size. Although this is visually indistinguishable from `text-transform: uppercase`, it is permitted behavior. Internet Explorer 5.x for Windows takes this approach.

It is possible that future versions of CSS will permit other variant types, but the specification does not hint at what these might be.

Examples

```
h1 {font-variant: small-caps;}
p {font-variant: normal;}
```

Related Properties

font

font-weight

`font-weight` alters the visual weight of characters in an element.

Summary

Value Syntax
normal | bold | bolder | lighter | 100 | 200 | 300 | 400 | 500 | 600 | 700 | 800 | 900 | inherit

Initial Value
normal

Percentages
n/a

Inherited
yes

Applies to
all elements

Media Groups
visual

Values

100
The font's characters should be lighter than those characters which result from a value of 200, or at a minimum have the same weight.

200
The font's characters should be at least as heavy as those characters which result from a value of 100, and should be heavier if possible.

300
The font's characters should be at least as heavy as those characters which result from a value of 200, and should be heavier if possible.

400
The font's characters should be at least as heavy as those characters which result from a value of 300, and should be heavier if possible.

500
The font's characters should be at least as heavy as those characters which result from a value of 400, and should be heavier if possible.

600
The font's characters should be at least as heavy as those characters which result from a value of 500, and should be heavier if possible.

700
The font's characters should be at least as heavy as those characters which result from a value of 600, and should be heavier if possible.

800
The font's characters should be at least as heavy as those characters which result from a value of 700, and should be heavier if possible.

900
The font's characters should be at least as heavy as those characters which result from a value of 800, and should be heavier if possible.

normal
Equivalent to the value 400.

bold
Equivalent to the value 700.

bolder

The font characters for the element should be heavier than those of the parent element. If there is a heavier font face available, use it; otherwise, increase the numeric keyword level by one. For example, if an element's parent has a weight of 400, and the element is set to `bolder`, then its weight will be 500 (assuming there is a heavier font face available). This may or may not have a visible effect. The weight of a font cannot be increased above 900.

lighter

The font characters for the element should be lighter than those of the parent element. If there is a lighter font face available, use it; otherwise, decrease the numeric keyword level by one. For example, if an element's parent has a weight of 400, and the element is set to `lighter`, then its weight will be 300 (assuming there is a heavier font face available). This may or may not have a visible effect. The weight of a font cannot be decreased below 100.

Notes

See the section on font rules in Chapter 1 for more details on font-weight assignment.

At sufficiently small font sizes, characters will be too small to show the effects of weighting. For example, with text eight pixels tall, there is little or no visual difference between normal and boldface text. This is due to the loss of legibility involved in boldfacing characters whose lines are only one or two pixels apart, and which are one pixel wide. Even though a piece of small text doesn't look heavy, it may in fact be as bold as possible, and many authors mistake the lack of visual change as a bug or an instance of missing support. In fact, it is a reflection of the limitations imposed by modern display environments.

In practice, a font will generally have at least two faces which the user agent recognizes: normal and bold. Some fonts may also contain light faces, but it is not certain that a user agent will recognize and use these faces.

Examples

```
strong {font-weight: bold;}
a:link, a:visited {font-weight: bolder;}
h3 {font-weight: 900;}
```

Related Properties

font

height

height defines the vertical distance between the top and bottom edges of the element's content area.

Summary

Value Syntax
<length> | <percentage> | auto | inherit

Initial Value
auto

Percentages
see "Values"

Inherited
no

Applies to
all elements except non-replaced inline elements, table columns, and column groups

Media Groups
visual

Values

<length>
Any length unit. Negative length values are not permitted for this property.

<percentage>
The height is calculated with respect to the height of the element's containing block, assuming that the containing block's height has been explicitly set. If not, then a percentage value is treated as auto.

auto
The result of this value depends on a number of factors. In the normal document flow, auto will result in whatever height is necessary to enclose the content of the element. In positioned

elements, it may have the same effect, or it may be overridden due to constraints introduced using properties such as `top` and `bottom`. See the section on positioning rules in Chapter 1 for more details.

Notes

If the height of a replaced element (e.g., an image) is set to a length unit, and no width is set, then the image will be scaled so that its height matches the declared value, and the width is altered by the same proportion. For example, an image 100 pixels tall and 50 pixels wide is set to `height: 200px`; thus its width will be increased to 100 pixels. Setting the height of a replaced element to a percentage will operate as described above, and make the height of the element some percentage of the height of its containing block. It is not possible to reduce an element to half its intrinsic size through a percentage value.

Examples

```
div.nav {position: fixed; top: 0; height: 15%;}
img.pic {height: 200px;}
select {height: 0.9em;}
```

Related Properties

`bottom`, `margin-bottom`, `margin-top`, `padding-bottom`, `padding-top`, `top`, `width`

left

`left` defines an offset of the left edge of an absolutely positioned element from the left edge of its positioning context, or the horizontal distance which a relatively positioned element will be displaced.

Summary

Value Syntax
`<length> | <percentage> | auto | inherit`

Initial Value
`auto`

Percentages
refer to width of containing block

Inherited
no

Applies to
positioned elements

Media Groups
visual

Values

<length>
A fixed distance from the bottom of the positioning context.

<percentage>
Some percentage of the width of the positioning context, assuming that the width of the context has been set explicitly. If not, then a percentage value for `left` is treated as though it were `auto`. In practice, this means that percentage values for `left` set on relatively positioned elements will be ignored.

auto
The actual distance which results will depend on a number of factors. These factors are the dimensions of horizontal measure for an absolutely positioned element (see the notes section). If the element has been relatively positioned, then `auto` has no apparent effect.

Notes

In the case of an absolutely positioned element, the horizontal dimensions of the element must add up to the width of the positioning context. If every measure of horizontal distance besides `left` is explicitly set, then a value of `auto` is changed to make sure that they all add up to the width of the positioning context. Similarly, in right-to-left writing modes such as Hebrew, if all of the horizontal dimensions including `left` are explicitly set, but do not add up to the width of the positioning context, then the value for `left` is discarded, and the necessary value is substituted. In both cases, a negative distance may be assigned to `left`. If `left` is set to `auto` in left-to-right writing modes such as English, then the left edge of the positioned element should be aligned with the place where it would have appeared had the element not been positioned.

In addition, setting `left` to `auto` may force other horizontal dimensions which are also set to `auto` to be reset to `0`. See the section on positioning calculations in Chapter 1 for more information.

In the case of relatively positioned elements, `left` defines a horizontal offset from the place where the relatively positioned element would ordinarily have appeared. Positive values for `left` will offset the element to the right, and negative values will move it to the left. In left-to-right writing modes such as English, if both `right` and `left` are set to explicit values, then the value for `right` will be discarded in favor of `left`.

Examples

```
div.sidebar {position: absolute; width: auto;
  left: 10%; right: 50%;}
em.slide-left { position: relative; left: -1em;}
```

Related Properties

```
bottom, position, right, top, width
```

letter-spacing

`letter-spacing` modifies the amount of space placed between adjacent characters.

Summary

Value Syntax
`normal | <length> | inherit`

Initial Value
`normal`

Percentages
n/a

Inherited
yes

Applies to
all elements

Media Groups
visual

Values

normal
The default spacing between letters is not changed. In practice, this is equivalent to setting the value to `0`.

<length>
This will add to the spacing between letters—the greater the length, the more space will be seen between letters. Negative values are permitted, and will cause letters to bunch together, to the point of potentially overwriting one another or even appearing to write text "backwards."

Notes

`letter-spacing` is treated as a modifier because in normal layout, there is no space between character boxes. The space normally seen between characters is an artifact of intentional design, as some amount of space is intentionally left to either side of a character glyph within its character box. This is done to prevent the glyphs from touching each other during rendering.

In fully justified text (see `text-align`), the space between letters may be programmatically altered in order to create the effect of full justification.

In order to preserve the relative spacing between characters for descendant elements, authors are encouraged to use `em` length units.

Examples
```
em {letter-spacing: 1px;}
h1.wider {letter-spacing: 0.5em;}
p.scrunched {letter-spacing: -0.5ex;}
table {letter-spacing: normal;}
```

Related Properties
`text-align`, `word-spacing`

line-height

`line-height` modifies the height of the inline boxes which make up a line of text.

Summary

Value Syntax
normal | <number> | <length> | <percentage> | inherit

Initial Value
normal

Percentages
refer to the font size of the element itself

Inherited
yes

Applies to
all elements

Media Groups
visual

Values

normal
Directs the user agent to set the height of lines in the element to a "reasonable" distance. This is recommended as a <number> value between 1.0 and 1.2, but user agents are free to use whatever value they choose.

<number>
The actual height of lines in the element is this value multiplied by the font-size of the element. In addition, the numeric value, and not the computed line-height, is inherited by any descendant elements. This allows descendants to have line-heights which are proportional to their font sizes. Use of this value is strongly encouraged. Negative values are not permitted.

<length>
The height of lines in the element is the value given. Note that this is actually a minimum height, as conditions within a given line may make its line-box taller than the length value given for line-height. Negative values are not permitted.

<percentage>
The height of lines in the element is calculated as a percentage of the element's font-size (*not* the parent element's font-size). Note that this is actually a minimum height, as conditions within a given line may make its line-box taller than the length value given for line-height. Negative values are not permitted.

Notes

The effects of `line-height` are actually far more complicated than they appear. The value of `line-height` for a given element is used to derive the half-leading which is applied to the top and bottom of each inline box in the line. These inline boxes are what collectively make up the line box. A line box may be taller than any of its constituent inline boxes, but it can never be shorter than the shortest inline box. It is also possible that the line box may be shorter than the contents of the line, in which case the contents may overlap the content of other lines. See the section on inline formatting in Chapter 1 for more details.

Support for `line-height` is less than exemplary in current Web browsers. Only with the advent of browsers such as Internet Explorer 5 for Macintosh and Opera 4 have Web browsers truly supported the line-height described in the CSS specification. Older browsers may evidence unexpected behaviors, generally in the form of pushing lines further apart than they should be drawn. In most cases, there is minimal impact on the layout (something which most authors will tolerate), but attempts at extreme typographic effects may be thwarted by browser limitations.

The height of marker boxes (see `display: marker`) is set using `line-height`.

The value of `line-height` can also be set as a part of the `font` property.

Examples

```
h1 {line-height: 130%;}
p {line-height: 1.1;}
pre {font-size: 10px; line-height: 11px;}
```

Related Properties

`font`, `font-size`, `vertical-align`

list-style

`list-style` is a shorthand property used to set the position and type of markers in a list; it can also be used to assign an image as the marker.

Summary

Value Syntax
```
[ <list-style-type> || <list-style-position> ||
<list-style-image> ] | inherit
```

Initial Value
not defined for shorthand properties

Percentages
n/a

Inherited
yes

Applies to
elements with a `display` of `list-item`

Media Groups
visual

Values

<list-style-type>
Any permitted value for the property `list-style-type`.

<list-style-position>
Any permitted value for the property `list-style-position`.

<list-style-image>
Any permitted value for the property `list-style-image`.

Notes
As with other shorthand properties, any unspecified keywords will reset the corresponding properties to their default values. See the section on shorthand properties in Chapter 1 for more details.

Examples
```
ol li {list-style: decimal;}
ul.state li {list-style: inside url(states/new-york.png);}
```

Related Properties
`list-style-image`, `list-style-position`, `list-style-type`

list-style-image

`list-style-image` defines a pointer to an image resource that is to be used as the marker for list items.

Summary

Value Syntax
`<uri> | none | inherit`

Initial Value
`none`

Percentages
n/a

Inherited
yes

Applies to
elements with a `display` of `list-item`

Media Groups
visual

Values

<uri>
A pointer to an image resource. If the URL cannot be resolved, then the property is treated as if the value were `none`.

none
No image should be used as a marker for the element.

Notes

Since it is not possible to affect the size of a marker image specified using `list-style-image`, authors should exercise caution to ensure that the image is not too large for the text in the list item's content. For more details on markers, refer to the entry for `marker` in the property `display`.

Note that since this property is inherited, a marker image set for a list will be applied to any lists which are descendants of the element.

The only way to prevent this is to set the value of `list-style-image` for these descendant lists to `none`.

Examples

```
ul.state li {list-style-image: url(states/new-york.png);}
ul.state li ul {list-style-image: none;}
```

Related Properties

`list-style`, `list-style-position`, `list-style-type`

list-style-position

`list-style-position` affects the placement of a marker in relation to the content of the list item.

Summary

Value Syntax
`inside | outside | inherit`

Initial Value
`outside`

Percentages
n/a

Inherited
yes

Applies to
elements with a `display` of `list-item`

Media Groups
visual

Values

inside
The marker is made an inline element at the beginning of the first line of the list item's content. This is somewhat similar to the effect created by `display: run-in`.

outside
The marker is placed outside the box containing the list item's content. The actual position of this marker is not specified. For

more flexible list-item markers, refer to the entry for the value `marker` in the property `display`.

Notes
Note that since this property is inherited, the marker position set for a list will be applied to any lists which are descendants of the element. The only way to prevent this is to set the value of `list-style-position` for these descendant lists to a different value.

Examples
```
ul.collapse {list-style-position: inside;}
ol li {list-style-position: outside;}
```

Related Properties
`list-style`, `list-style-image`, `list-style-type`

list-style-type

`list-style-type` sets the counting (or bullet) style used in the marker for a list item.

Summary

Value Syntax
disc | circle | square | decimal | decimal-leading-zero |
lower-roman | upper-roman | lower-greek | lower-alpha |
lower-latin | upper-alpha | upper-latin | hebrew | armenian |
georgian | cjk-ideographic | hiragana | katakana |
hiragana-iroha | katakana-iroha | none | inherit

Initial Value
disc

Percentages
n/a

Inherited
yes

Applies to
elements with a `display` of `list-item`

Media Groups
visual

Values

disc
Although the exact representation of this value is not specified, most user agents render it as a filled circle.

circle
Although the exact representation of this value is not specified, most user agents render it as an unfilled circle.

square
Although the exact representation of this value is not specified, most user agents render it as a square (oddly enough). However, some will fill the square, while others leave it unfilled.

decimal
Specifies a decimal counting system, beginning with *1* and proceeding to *2, 3, 4*, and so on.

decimal-leading-zero
Specifies a decimal counting system, beginning with *01* and proceeding to *02, 03, 04*, and so on. User agent may fill in enough leading zeros to match the number of digits in the last item; for example, a 320-item list might start with *001*. This behavior is not required.

lower-roman
Specifies counting with lowercase roman numerals, beginning with *i* and proceeding to *ii, iii, iv*, and so on.

upper-roman
Specifies counting with uppercase roman numerals, beginning with *I* and proceeding to *II, III, IV*, and so on.

lower-alpha
Specifies counting with lowercase ASCII letters, beginning with *a* and proceeding to *b, c, d*, and so on.

upper-alpha
Specifies counting with uppercase ASCII letters, beginning with *A* and proceeding to *B, C, D*, and so on.

lower-latin
Specifies counting with lowercase ASCII letters, beginning with *a* and proceeding to *b, c,* d, and so on.

upper-latin
Specifies counting with uppercase ASCII letters, beginning with
A and proceeding to *B*, *C*, *D*, and so on.

lower-greek
Specifies counting with classical Greek letters, beginning with
alpha and proceeding to *beta*, *gamma*, *delta*, and so on.

hebrew
Specifies counting in traditional Hebrew.

armenian
Specifies counting in traditional Armenian.

4

georgian
Specifies counting in traditional Georgian.

cjk-ideographic
Specifies counting in ideographic numbers.

hiragana
Specifies counting in the Japanese hiragana system, beginning
with *a* and proceeding to *i*, *u*, *e*, *o*, *ka*, *ki*, and so on.

katakana
Specifies counting in the Japanese katakana system, beginning
with *A* and proceeding to *I*, *U*, *E*, *O*, *KA*, *KI*, and so on.

hiragana-iroha
Specifies counting in the Japanese hiragana-iroha system,
beginning with *i* and proceeding to *ro*, *ha*, *ni*, *ho*, and so on.

katakana-iroha
Specifies counting in the Japanese katakana-iroha system,
beginning with *I* and proceeding to *RO*, *HA*, *NI*, *HO*, and so on.

none
No marker should be displayed.

Notes

If a user agent cannot support the counting system specified, it should
treat the value as `decimal`. List items within an ordered list always
increment the list's counter (see `counter-increment` for more
details) in decimal format, with the actual counter type being
translated from decimal to the declared type. Thus, the sixth list

item in an ordered list will typically have a counter value of 6; if the declared type is `lower-alpha`, then the 6 will be translated to an `f`. CSS does not specify how said translations should take place, and there is no provision for handling "wrap-around" in non-numeric counting systems. For example, the specification does not define the next entry after "Z" in an alphabetic counting system.

Note that the default value is `disc`, which applies even to list items in ordered lists. Thus, if a rule using `list-style` is applied to list items in an ordered list, and the value of `list-style` does not contain a list style type, the default value of `disc` will be used.

Note also that since this property is inherited; the marker style set for a list will be applied to any lists which are descendants of the element. The only way to prevent this is to set the value of `list-style-type` for these descendant lists to a different value.

Examples

```
ol.caesar {list-style-type: upper-roman;}
li.letter {list-style-type: lower-alpha;}
```

Related Properties

`list-style`, `list-style-image`, `list-style-position`

margin

`margin` is a shorthand property which sets the width of the margins on all four sides of an element.

Summary

Value Syntax
[<length> | <percentage> | auto]{1,4} | inherit

Initial Value
not defined for shorthand properties

Percentages
refer to width of containing block

Inherited
no

Applies to
all elements

Media Groups
visual

Values

<length>
Any length value.

<percentage>
The margin's width is calculated with respect to the width of the element's containing block (usually, but not always, the content area of the parent element).

auto
Sets the values for all four margins to be automatically calculated. This will have different meanings for each side; for more details, refer to the individual margin properties, or the section on height and width calculations in Chapter 1.

Notes

Length and percentage values may be mixed together. If there are four values declared, they apply in the order: top, right, bottom, left. In the case of three values, the first will apply to the top margin, the second to the left and right margins, and the third to the bottom margin. If two values are declared, the first applies to the top and bottom margins, while the second applies to the left and right margins. If one value is declared, it applies to all four margins.

Vertically adjacent margins will collapse to the larger of the two. See the section on the box model in Chapter 1 for more details.

For the effects of margins on inline elements, refer to the individual margin properties.

Examples
```
h1 {margin: 1.5em 5% 0.5em;}
img {margin: 10px;}
a.external:link {margin: 1em;}
```

Related Properties
```
margin-bottom, margin-left, margin-right, margin-top
```

margin-bottom

`margin-bottom` sets the width of the margin on the bottom of an element.

Summary

Value Syntax
[<length> | <percentage> | auto] | inherit

Initial Value
0

Percentages
refer to width of containing block

Inherited
no

Applies to
all elements

Media Groups
visual

Values

<length>
Any length value.

<percentage>
The margin's width is calculated with respect to the width of the element's containing block (usually, but not always, the content area of the parent element).

auto
This value will have different effects depending on the situation. For floated elements, block-level elements in the normal flow, relatively positioned elements, and inline-level elements, replaced or otherwise, `auto` is equivalent to 0. For other circumstances, see the section on height calculations in Chapter 1.

Notes

If two elements which are vertically adjacent (that is, they follow one another in the normal flow of the document) have margins set, then the actual distance between the two borders of the two elements is equal to the larger of the margins. Thus, if an element with a `margin-bottom` of `1.5em` is immediately followed by an element with a `margin-top` of `1em`, the distance between the borders of the two elements will be `1.5em`. See the section on the box model in Chapter 1 for more details.

`margin-bottom` has no effect on non-replaced inline elements. User agents should assign the value of `margin-bottom` to these elements, but since inline margins have no impact on line height calculations, there will be no visible effect. This is not the case with replaced inline elements, which have the bottom margin as part of their element box.

Examples

```
h1 {margin-bottom: 0.33em;}
table {margin-bottom: 3%;}
img.drop {margin-bottom: 12px;}
```

Related Properties

`margin, margin-left, margin-right, margin-top`

margin-left

`margin-left` sets the width of the margin on the left side of an element.

Summary

Value Syntax
`[ <length> | <percentage> | auto ] | inherit`

Initial Value
`0`

Percentages
refer to width of containing block

Inherited
no

Applies to
all elements

Media Groups
visual

Values

<length>
Any length value.

<percentage>
The margin's width is calculated with respect to the width of the element's containing block (usually, but not always, the content area of the parent element).

auto
This value will have different effects depending on the situation. For floated elements, relatively positioned elements, and inline-level elements, replaced or otherwise, `auto` is equivalent to 0. For other circumstances, see the section on width calculations in Chapter 1.

Notes

`margin-left` will have an effect on the layout of inline elements. In the case of replaced element-like images, the margin is rendered as part of the element box. In the case of non-replaced elements like hyperlinks, the left margin is applied to the left side of the element. If the inline element is broken across two or more lines, the left margin is applied to the left side of the element on the *first* line in which it appears, and is *not* applied to the left sides of the element in subsequent lines. Horizontally adjacent margins do not collapse; see the section on the box model in Chapter 1 for more details.

Examples

```
h2 {margin-left: 25px;}
pre {margin-left: 3em;}
li {margin-left: 7%;}
```

Related Properties

`margin, margin-bottom, margin-right, margin-top`

margin-right

`margin-right` sets the width of the margin on the right side of an element.

Summary

Value Syntax
[<length> | <percentage> | auto] | inherit

Initial Value
0

Percentages
refer to width of containing block

Inherited
no

Applies to
all elements

Media Groups
visual

Values

<length>
Any length value.

<percentage>
The margin's width is calculated with respect to the width of the element's containing block (usually, but not always, the content area of the parent element).

auto
This value will have different effects depending on the situation. For floated elements, relatively positioned elements, and inline-level elements, replaced or otherwise, auto is equivalent to 0. For other circumstances, see the section on width calculations in Chapter 1.

Notes

margin-right will have an effect on the layout of inline elements. In the case of replaced element-like images, the margin is rendered as part of the element box. In the case of non-replaced elements like hyperlinks, the right margin is applied to the right side of the element. If the inline element is broken across two or more lines, the right margin is applied to the right side of the element on the *last* line in which it appears, and is *not* applied to the right sides of the element in preceding lines. Horizontally adjacent margins do not collapse; see the section on the box model in Chapter 1 for more details.

Examples

```
h3 {margin-left: 5%;}
blockquote {margin-right: 5em;}
li {margin-right: auto;}
```

Related Properties

`margin, margin-bottom, margin-left, margin-top`

margin-top

`margin-top` sets the width of the margin on the top of an element.

Summary

Value Syntax
[<length> | <percentage> | auto] | inherit

Initial Value
0

Percentages
refer to width of containing block

Inherited
no

Applies to
all elements

Media Groups
visual

Values

<length>
Any length value.

<percentage>
The margin's width is calculated with respect to the width of the element's containing block (usually, but not always, the content area of the parent element).

auto

This value will have different effects depending on the situation. For floated elements, block-level elements in the normal flow, relatively positioned elements, and inline-level elements, replaced or otherwise, `auto` is equivalent to `0`. For other circumstances, see the section on height calculations in Chapter 1.

Notes

If two elements which are vertically adjacent (that is, they follow one another in the normal flow of the document) have margins set, then the actual distance between the two borders of the two elements is equal to the larger of the margins. Thus, if an element with a `margin-top` of `1.75em` is immediately preceded by an element with a `margin-bottom` of `1em`, the distance between the borders of the two elements will be `1.75em`. See the section on the box model in Chapter 1 for more details.

`margin-top` has no visible effect on non-replaced inline elements. User agents should assign the value of `margin-top` to these elements, but since inline margins have no impact on line height calculations, there will be no visible effect. This is not the case with replaced inline elements, which render the top margin as part of their element box.

Examples

```
h4 {margin-top: 1.5em;}
table {margin-top: 4%;}
img.drop {margin-top: 12px;}
```

Related Properties

`margin`, `margin-bottom`, `margin-left`, `margin-right`

marker-offset

`marker-offset` defines the distance between the nearest border edges of a marker and its associated principal box.

Summary

Value Syntax

`<length> | auto | inherit`

Initial Value

`auto`

Percentages
n/a

Inherited
no

Applies to
elements with a `display` of `marker`

Media Groups
visual

Values

<length>
Any length value. This sets the distance between the marker's edge and the nearest edge of the principal box. Negative values are permitted.

auto
The distance between the marker's edge and the nearest edge of the principal box is determined by the user agent.

Notes

For more details on markers, refer to the entry for `marker` in the property `display`.

Examples

```
li:before {display: marker; marker-offset: 1.25em;
    width: 30px; content: url(spiral.jpg);}
p.aside:after {display: marker; marker-offset: 10px;
    content: " (End of aside.)";}
```

Related Properties

display

max-height

`max-height` sets an upper bound on the height of an element.

Summary

Value Syntax
`<length> | <percentage> | none | inherit`

Initial Value
none

Percentages
refer to height of containing block

Inherited
no

Applies to
all elements except non-replaced inline elements and table elements

Media Groups
visual

4

Values

<length>
Any length unit. The element can never have a value for `height` which exceeds this distance.

<percentage>
Limits the element's height to be at most this percentage of the height of the containing block. If the containing block's height changes— due to document reflow triggered by a change in the default font size, for example—then the maximum height of the element will change with it.

none
There is no limit to the height of the element.

Notes
See the section on calculating element heights in Chapter 1 for more details on how `max-height` affects layout.

Examples
```
img {max-height: 40px;}
p.aside {max-height: 10em;}
div.sidebar {max-height: 50%;}
```

Related Properties
`height`, `min-height`

max-width

`max-width` sets an upper bound on the width of an element.

Summary

Value Syntax
<length> | <percentage> | none | inherit

Initial Value
none

Percentages
refer to width of containing block

Inherited
no

Applies to
all elements except non-replaced inline elements and table elements

Media Groups
visual

Values

<length>
Any length unit. The element can never have a value for `width` which exceeds this distance.

<percentage>
Limits the element's width to be at most this percentage of the width of the containing block. If the containing block's width changes—due to document reflow triggered by a change in the size of the browser window, for example—then the maximum width of the element will change with it.

none
There is no limit to the width of the element.

Notes

See the section on calculating element widths in Chapter 1 for more details on how `max-width` affects layout.

Examples

```
p {max-width: 90%;}
img.sidefig {max-width: 200px;}
div.sidebar {max-width: 20em;}
```

Related Properties

min-width, width

min-height

4

min-height sets a lower bound on the height of an element.

Summary

Value Syntax
<length> | <percentage> | inherit

Initial Value
0

Percentages
refer to height of containing block

Inherited
no

Applies to
all elements except non-replaced inline elements and table elements

Media Groups
visual

Values

<length>
Any length unit. The element can never have a value for height
which is lower than this distance.

<percentage>
Limits the element's height to be at least this percentage of the
height of the containing block. If the containing block's height
changes—due to document reflow triggered by a change in the
default font size, for example—then the minimum height of the
element will change with it.

Notes
See the section on calculating element heights in Chapter 1 for more details on how `min-height` affects layout.

Examples
```
div.top {min-height: 85px;}
img {min-height: 10px;}
h1 {min-height: 1em;}
```

Related Properties
`height`, `max-height`

min-width

`min-width` sets a lower bound on the width of an element.

Summary

Value Syntax
`<length> | <percentage> | inherit`

Initial Value
UA dependent

Percentages
refer to width of containing block

Inherited
no

Applies to
all elements except non-replaced inline elements and table elements

Media Groups
visual

Values

<length>
Any length unit. The element can never have a value for `width` which is less than this distance.

<percentage>
Limits the element's width to be at least this percentage of the width of the containing block. If the containing block's width changes—due to document reflow triggered by a change in the

size of the browser window, for example—then the maximum width of the element will change with it.

Notes
See the section on calculating element widths in Chapter 1 for more details on how `max-width` affects layout.

Examples
```
p {min-width: 10em;}
img {min-width: 25px;}
h2 {min-width: 50%;}
```

Related Properties
`max-width`, `width`

outline

`outline` is a shorthand property which is used to set the width, color, and style of an outline around an element.

Summary

Value Syntax
`[ <outline-color> || <outline-style> || <outline-width> ] | inherit`

Initial Value
not defined for shorthand properties

Percentages
n/a

Inherited
no

Applies to
all elements

Media Groups
visual, interactive

Values

<outline-color>
Any permitted value of the property `outline-color`.

<outline-style>
Any permitted value of the property `outline-style`.

<outline-width>
Any permitted value of the property `outline-width`.

Notes

An outline is usually applied to an element when it has focus (i.e., is the current subject of user interaction). However, there is no restriction on the type or state of elements to which outlines may be applied. An outline could be drawn around every paragraph just as easily as around the link which has focus. Outlines are drawn along the outside edge of the element's borders, and do not trigger reflow of the document when they are drawn or removed. Thus, they may be drawn over the background, or (if wide enough) even the borders, background, or content of other elements.

Examples

```
a:hover {outline: 1px dotted invert;}
input:focus {outline: blue 0.5ex outset;}
h1 {outline: purple solid 1em;}
```

Related Properties

`:focus, outline-color, outline-style, outline-width`

outline-color

`outline-color` sets the color for an outline around an element.

Summary

Value Syntax
`<color> | invert | inherit`

Initial Value
`invert`

Percentages
n/a

Inherited
no

Applies to
all elements

Media Groups
visual, interactive

Values

<color>
Any color value.

invert
The outline performs a color inversion of the area where it is drawn. This is analogous to a "reverse video" effect, and ensures that the outline will be visible regardless of the background color(s) behind it.

4

Notes

Unlike the element's border, an outline can only have one color.

Because outlines can overwrite other elements, as well as any backgrounds behind the element to which the outline is applied, authors are encouraged to use the color keyword `invert` whenever possible.

Examples

```
input:focus {outline-color: invert;}
h1.high {outline-color: invert;}
```

Related Properties

`:focus, outline, outline-style, outline-width`

outline-style

`outline-style` determines the style of an outline around an element.

Summary

Value Syntax
`none | dotted | dashed | solid | double | groove | ridge | inset | outset | inherit`

Initial Value
`none`

Percentages
`n/a`

Inherited
no

Applies to
all elements

Media Groups
visual, interactive

Values

none
No outline is drawn. The primary side effect of this value is that the computed `outline-width` for the outline in question will be set to `0`.

dotted
The outline is drawn as a series of dots. The specific placement of these dots is left to the user agent.

dashed
The outline is drawn as a series of short line segments. The specific placement of these lines is left to the user agent.

solid
The outline is drawn as a single unbroken line.

double
The outline is drawn as a pair of unbroken lines. The specific placement of these lines, including the separation between them, is left to the user agent.

groove
The outline is drawn as though it were a furrow carved into the surface of the document. This implies a "shading" of the outline, but the CSS specification does not describe this in detail. Most user agents handle this shading by splitting each outline into two adjacent lines, and darkening the upper (or leftward) half while lightening the lower (or rightward) half of each outline.

ridge
The outline is drawn as though it were a ridge pushing up the surface of the document. This implies a "shading" of the outline, but the CSS specification does not describe this in detail. Most user agents handle this shading by splitting each outline into two adjacent lines, and lightening the upper (or leftward) half while darkening the lower (or rightward) half of each outline.

inset

The outline is drawn as though the entire element is pushing the surface of the document away from the user. This implies a "shading" of the outline, but the CSS specification does not describe this in detail. Most user agents handle this shading by lightening the bottom and right outlines while darkening the top and left outlines.

outset

The outline is drawn as though the entire element is pushing the surface of the document toward the user. This implies a "shading" of the outline, but the CSS specification does not describe this in detail. Most user agents handle this shading by darkening the bottom and right outlines while lightening the top and left outlines.

4

Notes

The value `hidden`, which is permitted for border styles, is not allowed for outline styles.

Examples

```
a:visited:focus {outline-style: dotted;}
pre.example {outline-style: outset;}
```

Related Properties

`:focus`, `outline`, `outline-color`, `outline-width`

outline-width

`outline-width` defines the width of the outline around an element.

Summary

Value Syntax
`<length> | thin | medium | thick | inherit`

Initial Value
medium

Percentages
n/a

Inherited
no

Applies to
all elements

Media Groups
visual, interactive

Values

<length>
Any length unit. Length units for this property may not be negative.

thin
An outline which is thinner than an outline set to `medium`.
The exact width is not defined by the CSS specification.

medium
An outline which is thicker than an outline set to `thin`, and thinner
than an outline set to `thick`. The exact width is not defined by the
CSS specification.

thick
An outline which is thicker than an outline set to `medium`.
The exact width is not defined by the CSS specification.

Notes
Because outlines can overwrite other elements, as well as any
backgrounds behind the element to which the outline is applied,
authors are encouraged to make their outlines as thin as possible.
This will minimize the chances of the outline overwriting and
obscuring useful content.

Examples
```
a:link:hover{outline-width: 2px;}
select {outline-width: 0;}
input:focus {outline-width: thick;}
```

Related Properties
`:focus, outline, outline-color, outline-style`

overflow

`overflow` determines how content which overflows its element's
content area should be handled.

Summary

Value Syntax
visible | hidden | scroll | auto | inherit

Initial Value
visible

Percentages
n/a

Inherited
no

Applies to
block-level and replaced elements

Media Groups
visual

Values

visible
Overflowing content should be displayed. The width of the content will be rendered as if the element were tall enough to contain all of the content, but the element's visible box will not be altered. This will give the effect of the content "spilling out" of its element's content area. The overflowing content will almost certainly overlap portions of the padding, borders, and margins of its containing element, and may in fact overlap parts of other elements.

hidden
Overflowing content should not be displayed. The region beyond which it is hidden is defined by the value of the property `clip`.

scroll
Overflowing content should not be displayed, but the user agent should provide some means of accessing the hidden content (e.g., a set of scrollbars). The region beyond which the content is not shown is defined by the value of the property `clip`. Furthermore, the CSS2 specification recommends that this value should always cause the scrolling mechanism to be rendered, regardless of whether it is actually needed.

auto
The behavior caused by this value is dependent on the user agent. The CSS2 specification recommends that if any content overflows, it should be accessible with a scrolling mechanism.

Notes
As of this writing, support for `overflow` is not very good. Of the known browsers, only Navigator 6 comes close to properly supporting this property.

Examples
```
div.inset {overflow: scroll;}
td {overflow: hidden;}
p.aside {overflow: scroll;}
```

Related Properties
`clip`

padding

`padding` is a shorthand property which is used to set the padding on all four sides of an element.

Summary

Value Syntax
```
[ <length> | <percentage> ]{1,4} | inherit
```

Initial Value
not defined for shorthand properties

Percentages
refer to width of containing block

Inherited
no

Applies to
all elements

Media Groups
visual

Values

<length>
Any length value. Negative length values are not permitted for the property.

The padding width is calculated with respect to the width of the element's containing block (usually, but not always, the content area of the parent element).

Notes

Length and percentage values may be mixed together. If there are four values declared, they apply in the order: top, right, bottom, left. In the case of three values, the first will apply to the top padding, the second to the left and right padding, and the third to the bottom padding. If two values are declared, the first applies to the top and bottom padding, while the second applies to the left and right padding. If one value is declared, it applies to all four padding.

For the effects of padding on inline elements, refer to the individual padding properties.

Examples

```
td {padding: 0.75ex;}
div.aside {padding: 1em 10px;}
h2 {padding: 0.5em 5% 0.25em 15px;}
```

Related Properties

padding-bottom, padding-left, padding-right, padding-top

padding-bottom

padding-bottom sets the width of the padding on the bottom of an element.

Summary

Value Syntax
[<length> | <percentage>] | inherit

Initial Value
0

Percentages
refer to width of containing block

Inherited
no

Applies to
all elements

Media Groups
visual

Values

<length>
Any length value. Negative length values are not permitted for this property.

<percentage>
The bottom padding's width is calculated with respect to the width of the element's containing block (usually, but not always, the content area of the parent element).

Notes

`padding-bottom` may or may not have an effect on non-replaced (e.g., text) inline elements. User agents should assign the value of `padding-bottom` to these elements, and it may increase the amount of background which is drawn. Any borders set on the element will also be pushed away from the content of the element. User agents are not, however, required to increase the visible background area of inline elements. Even if the user agent does increase the visible background, it may or may not overwrite content in following lines. Authors are thus encouraged to avoid setting bottom padding on inline elements.

Examples

```
h3 {padding-bottom: 5px;}
ul {padding-bottom: 1.5em;}
```

Related Properties

padding, padding-left, padding-right, padding-top

padding-left

`padding-left` sets the width of the padding on the left side of an element.

Summary

Value Syntax
[<length> | <percentage>] | inherit

Initial Value
0

Percentages
refer to width of containing block

Inherited
no

Applies to
all elements

Media Groups
visual

Values

<length>
Any length value.

<percentage>
The left padding's width is calculated with respect to the width of the element's containing block (usually, but not always, the content area of the parent element).

Notes

padding-left will have an effect on the layout of inline elements. In the case of non-replaced elements like hyperlinks, the left padding is applied to the left side of the element, and will extend the visible background of the element. It will also push the border away from the element's content. If the inline element is broken across two or more lines, the left padding is applied to the left side of the element on the *first* line in which it appears, and is *not* applied to the left sides of the element in subsequent lines.

Examples

```
h2 {padding-left: 20px;}
pre {padding-left: 2em;}
div.column {padding-left: 10%;}
```

Related Properties
padding, padding-bottom, padding-right, padding-top

padding-right

padding-right sets the width of the padding on the right side of
an element.

Summary

Value Syntax
[<length> | <percentage>] | inherit

Initial Value
0

Percentages
refer to width of containing block

Inherited
no

Applies to
all elements

Media Groups
visual

Values

<length>
Any length value.

<percentage>
The right padding's width is calculated with respect to the width
of the element's containing block (usually, but not always, the
content-area of the parent element).

Notes

padding-right will have an effect on the layout of inline elements.
In the case of non-replaced elements like hyperlinks, the right
padding is applied to the right side of the element, and will extend
the visible background of the element. It will also push the border
away from the element's content. If the inline element is broken
across two or more lines, the right padding is applied to the right

side of the element on the *last* line in which it appears, and is *not* applied to the right sides of the element in following lines.

Examples

```
h1 {padding-right: 5%;}
p.example {padding-right: 40px;}
```

Related Properties

padding, padding-bottom, padding-left, padding-top

padding-top

padding-top sets the width of the padding on the top of an element.

Summary

Value Syntax
[<length> | <percentage>] | inherit

Initial Value
0

Percentages
refer to width of containing block

Inherited
no

Applies to
all elements

Media Groups
visual

Values

<length>
Any length value.

<percentage>
The padding's width is calculated with respect to the width of the element's containing block (usually, but not always, the content area of the parent element).

Notes

`padding-top` may or may not have an effect on non-replaced (e.g., text) inline elements. User agents should assign the value of `padding-top` to these elements, and it may increase the amount of background which is drawn. Any borders set on the element will also be pushed away from the content of the element. User agents are not, however, required to increase the visible background area of inline elements. Even if the user agent does increase the visible background, it may or may not overwrite content in preceding lines. Authors are thus encouraged to avoid setting top padding on inline elements.

Examples

```
h3 {padding-top: 8px;}
pre.code {padding-top: 0.5em;}
```

Related Properties

`padding`, `padding-bottom`, `padding-left`, `padding-right`

position

`position` determines the method by which an element's box is laid out.

Summary

Value Syntax
static | relative | absolute | fixed | inherit

Initial Value
static

Percentages
n/a

Inherited
no

Applies to
all elements, but not to generated content

Media Groups
visual

Values

static

The element box is laid out as a part of the normal document flow, following the preceding element and preceding following elements. Its content will flow around any floated elements. If an element is set to this type of positioning, any values for `left` and `top` will be ignored.

relative

The element's box is laid out as a part of the normal flow, and then offset by some distance. The offset distance is declared through some combination of the properties `left`, `right`, `top` and `bottom`; if these all have a value of `0`, then the box is not offset. The space which the element would normally have occupied is preserved, and other elements in the document are laid out as though the relatively positioned element were still a part of the normal flow. It is possible that the relatively positioned element will overlap other elements. A relatively positioned element, even one which is not offset, establishes a containing block for its descendant elements.

absolute

The element's box is laid out in relation to its containing block, and is entirely removed from the normal flow of the document. The containing block of an absolutely positioned element is the nearest ancestor element with a `position` other than `static`. If no such ancestor exists, then the containing block is the root element of the document. The edges of the absolutely positioned element's box are positioned via the properties `left`, `right`, `top` and `bottom`, which specify offsets from the edges of the containing block. The space which the element would have occupied had it remained in the normal flow is closed up as though the element did not exist, and other elements are laid out as though the absolutely positioned element did not exist. Care must be taken to ensure that the positioned element does not overlap other elements. Since the containing block will always be some element within the document, or the root element, an absolutely positioned element will scroll with the rest of the document.

fixed

The element's box is absolutely positioned, with all of the behaviors which are described for `position: absolute`. The major difference is that the containing block of a fixed-position element is always the viewport. In Web browsers, this would be the browser window, and so a fixed-position element will not scroll with the rest of the document. In paged media, each page is a viewport. Thus, a fixed-position element in paged media will appear on every page, which can be used to simulate effects such as running footers. See Chapter 6 for more details.

Notes

A common method of establishing a containing block for absolutely positioned elements is to set an ancestor element to `position: relative` with no offsets. This will cause no visible change to the relatively positioned ancestor, but will define the desired containing block for any descendant elements.

Examples

```
img#lead {position: absolute;}
div.top {position: fixed; top: 0; height: 10% width: 100%;}
sup {position: relative; bottom: 0.66em;}
```

Related Properties

`bottom, left, right, top, z-index`

quotes

`quotes` is used to define the quotation pairs which are used at each level of nested quotation.

Summary

Value Syntax
`[<string> <string>]+ | none | inherit`

Initial Value
UA dependent

Percentages
n/a

Inherited
yes

Applies to
all elements

Media Groups
visual

Values

\<string> \<string>

A pair of string values which are used to represent the open- and close-quotes. These are always in the order of open-quote first, and close-quote second. The first pair of marks is used for the first (or outermost) level of quotation, the second pair for the next level of nested quotation, and so on. An arbitrary number of quotation pairs may be supplied. Single-quote marks may be enclosed by double-quote marks, and vice versa.

none

This prevents the values `open-quote` and `close-quote` on the property `content` from generating any quotation marks.

Notes

Although this property can be used to create customized quotation schemes, it is most useful for supplying quotation schemes for languages which the user agent may not recognize.

Examples

```
blockquote {quotes: '"' '"' "'" "'";}
q:lang(fr) {quotes: "<<" ">>" "<" ">";}
```

Related Properties

`content`

right

`right` defines an offset of the right edge of an absolutely positioned element from the right edge of its positioning context, or the horizontal distance which a relatively positioned element will be displaced.

Summary

Value Syntax

`<length> | <percentage> | auto | inherit`

Initial Value

`auto`

Percentages

refer to width of containing block

Inherited
no

Applies to
positioned elements

Media Groups
visual

Values

<length>
A fixed distance from the bottom of the positioning context.

<percentage>
Some percentage of the width of the positioning context, assuming
that the width of the context has been set explicitly. If not, then a
percentage value for right is treated as though it were auto. In
practice, this means that percentage values for right set on relatively
positioned elements will be ignored.

auto
The actual distance which results will depend on a number of factors.
These factors are the dimensions of horizontal measure for an
absolutely positioned element (see the notes section). If the element
has been relatively positioned, then auto has no apparent effect.

Notes

In the case of an absolutely positioned element, the horizontal
dimensions of the element must add up to the width of the
positioning context. If every measure of horizontal distance
besides right is explicitly set, then a value of auto is changed
to make sure that they all add up to the width of the positioning
context. Similarly, in left-to-right writing modes such as English,
if all of the horizontal dimensions including right are explicitly
set, but do not add up to the width of the positioning context,
then the value for right is discarded, and the necessary value is
substituted. In both cases, a negative distance may be assigned to
right. If right is set to auto in right-to-left writing modes such as
Hebrew, then the right edge of the positioned element should be
aligned with the place where it would have appeared had the element
not been positioned.

In addition, setting right to auto may force other horizontal
dimensions which are also set to auto to be reset to 0. See the
section on positioning calculations in Chapter 1 for more information.

In the case of relatively positioned elements, `right` defines a horizontal offset from the place where the relatively positioned element would ordinarily have appeared. Positive values for `right` will offset the element to the right, and negative values will move it to the right. In right-to-left writing modes such as Hebrew, if both `right` and `left` are set to explicit values, then the value for `left` will be discarded in favor of `right`.

Examples

```
div.sidebar {position: absolute; width: auto;
   left: 10%; right: 50%;}
em.slide-right { position: relative; right: -1em;}
```

Related Properties

`bottom`, `left`, `position`, `top`, `width`

table-layout

`table-layout` determines the layout method used in rendering a table.

Summary

Value Syntax
`auto | fixed | inherit`

Initial Value
`auto`

Percentages
n/a

Inherited
no

Applies to
elements with a `display` of `table` or `inline-table`

Media Groups
visual

Values

auto
The table should be laid out according to some automatic layout algorithm. There is a suggested algorithm given in the CSS

specification, but the specification does not require that a particular algorithm be used, so it is up to each user agent to implement its own method.

fixed

The table should be laid out according to the provided fixed-table layout method. This method states that the table's width is given with the property `width`. If the value given for `width` is `auto`, then the value for `table-layout` is changed to `auto`. If not, then column widths are determined by the following rules:

- If the column element has a `width` other than `auto`, then the declared value sets the width of the column.

- If the column's `width` is set to `auto`, then the first cell in the column which does not have `width: auto` will set the width of the column. If that cell spans multiple columns, then its width is divided evenly between the spanned columns.

- Any remaining columns will evenly divide the amount of horizontal space available, subtracting any borders or cell spacing.

Once these steps are performed, then the width of the table is either the value of the property `width` set on the table, or the sum of the width of all the columns, borders, and cell spacing, whichever is greater. If the table's width exceeds that of its columns, then all columns should be widened equally until the aggregate column, border, and cell spacing widths equal the width of the table. Once the table has been laid out, any content which cannot fit into its cell will overflow according to the value of the property `overflow`. Since the specification does not say anything about the height of rows, it will be up to user agents to invent their own solutions, which may vary.

Notes

The CSS specification provides an algorithm for calculating cell and row heights which does not depend on the width algorithms described above. In summary, a row's height is largely dependent upon the cells within that row. A table row must be at least as tall as the tallest cell in that row, regardless of any value assigned to the row element's `height`. Similarly, any cell must be tall enough to display all of its content, regardless of any value assigned to the cell element's `height`.

However, the specification does not say what should happen in the following circumstance:

- The table's declared height does not equal the aggregate height of the rows, borders, and cell spacing.

  Nor does it explain the following:

- The meaning of percentage values assigned to the property `height` when set on table cells, table rows, or table row groups.

- The effect that cells which span multiple rows will have on row-height calculations, except to say that the row heights must add up to a height tall enough to contain the spanning cell.

Given these ambiguities, authors should expect that user agents will differ in their handling of height calculations for tables.

Examples

```
table.granite {table-layout: fixed;}
table {table-layout: auto;}
```

Related Properties

`border-collapse`, `cell-spacing`, `empty-cells`

text-align

`text-align` determines the way in which line boxes are aligned within a block-level element.

Summary

Value Syntax
left | right | center | justify | <string> | inherit

Initial Value
depends on UA and writing direction

Percentages
n/a

Inherited
yes

Applies to
block-level elements (except the value `<string>`, which applies only to table cells)

Media Groups
visual

Values

left
The left edge of each line box is aligned with the left edge of the block-level element's content area.

right
The right edge of each line box is aligned with the right edge of the block-level element's content area.

center
The center of each line box is aligned with the center of the block-level element's content area.

justify
The edges of each line box should align with the edges of the block-level element's content area. This may be accomplished by programmatically increasing the letter- and word-spacing of text within a given line, but the CSS specification does not require a particular method. User agents are permitted to interpret this value as either `left` or `right`, depending on the writing direction for the element.

<string>
The content of cells in a column will align on the given string. This value may be applied only to table cells; if set on other types of elements, the value is treated as either `left` or `right`, depending on the writing direction for the element. As of this writing, no known user agent supports this value.

Notes

The value `justify` provides the effect of "full justification" or "double justification," which is a time-honored way of laying out text in print media. However, fully justified text can actually be more difficult to read on a computer screen, so authors are urged to use `justify` with caution.

Examples

```
p.column {text-align: justify;}
td.total {text-align: ".";}
div.rightside {text-align: right;}
```

Related Properties

direction, letter-spacing, word-spacing

text-decoration

text-decoration is used to add "decorations" to inline content.

Summary

Value Syntax
none | [underline || overline || line-through || blink] |
inherit

Initial Value
none

Percentages
n/a

Inherited
no

Applies to
all elements

Media Groups
visual

Values

none
No decoration should be added to the inline text.

underline
An underline is drawn beneath the inline text.

overline
An overline is drawn above the inline text.

line-through

A line should be drawn through the middle of the inline text. Note that "middle" does not imply "vertical center," as the line will most likely be drawn closer to the center of lowercase characters than the actual center of the character boxes.

blink

The inline text should blink on and off, analogous to the `BLINK` element introduced by Netscape. User agents are not required to support this value.

Notes

If this property is set on a block-level element, it will actually affect the inline content of the element.

The color of any text decoration is set by the foreground color of the text. However, it is not always the case that the color of an element will match the color of the text decoration near it. This can occur due to the "spanning" of an element by the decoration set on an ancestor element.

A text decoration is not inherited by descendant elements. However, the decoration set on an element will affect the entire element, including any descendants. Consider a hyperlink which has been set to `text-decoration: underline`. Within the hyperlink is an `EM` element. Since the `EM` does not inherit the decoration, its value for text-decoration is none. The underline still continues underneath the `EM`, however, since it is a descendant of the hyperlink. This is referred to as the "spanning" of descendant elements by a text decoration.

This has some interesting consequences. Take the hyperlink-`EM` example, and assume that the hyperlink and its underline are colored blue, while the `EM` is colored red. The hyperlink's underline will be blue, even when it appears beneath the red `EM` element. Thus, it is possible for a text decoration's color to be different than the color of the text near it. It is also possible for a decoration to cut through text. Take an underlined element which contains a `SUB` (subscript) element. The subscripted text will be lowered with respect to its parent element's text, but the parent's underline will not change position. Thus the subscripted text will likely overlap the underline.

If an element contains no text, then this property is ignored. Thus, it is not possible to underline an image by using `text-decoration`. However, images may have underlines appear beneath them due to the "spanning" described earlier.

In many Web browsers, setting an element's `text-decoration` value to `none` will prevent the display of any decorations within that element, even if it should have been spanned by the decoration of a parent element. The exceptions are Internet Explorer 5 for Macintosh, Navigator 6, and Opera 4+ (although Opera still does not span decorations across images).

Examples
```
a[href] {text-decoration: underline;}
p.old {text-decoration: line-through;}
blink {text-decoration: blink;}
```

4

Related Properties
None.

text-indent

`text-indent` defines an indentation distance for the first line of text in a block-level element.

Summary

Value Syntax
`<length> | <percentage> | inherit`

Initial Value
0

Percentages
refer to width of containing block

Inherited
yes

Applies to
block-level elements

Media Groups
visual

Values

<length>
Any length value. Negative lengths are permitted for the property, and will produce a "hanging indent" effect. Authors should be sure to increase the element's margin so that the hanging indent can

still be seen, especially if the edge of the element is close to the edge of the viewport.

<percentage>
The first line of text is indented by a distance relative to the width of the element's containing block. The computed indentation will be the same regardless of the width of the element, so it is possible to specify an indentation which is greater than the width of the element. The CSS specification does not say what should happen in such cases.

Notes
`text-indent` is a simple way to produce the "tabbed first line" effect common in print media.

Examples
```
p {text-indent: 3em;}
div.hang {text-indent: -40px; margin-left: 40px;}
p.odd {text-indent: 50%;}
```

Related Properties
None

text-shadow

`text-shadow` specifies one or more shadows which are derived from the text of an element.

Summary

Value Syntax
```
none | [<color> || <length> <length> <length>? ,]*
[<color> || <length> <length> <length>?] | inherit
```

Initial Value
none

Percentages
n/a

Inherited
no

Applies to
all elements

Media Groups
visual

Values

none
No shadows should be associated with the element.

<color>
Any color value. This gives the color of the shadow. If no color is provided, the shadow's color is taken from the value of the property `color` for the element.

<length> <length> <length>
The offset distances and blur radius for the shadow, in the order *x-offset*, *y-offset*, and *blur radius*. The two offset values are required for any shadow, but the blur radius is optional. Negative values are permitted for the offset lengths, but not the blur radius. A negative x-offset will place the shadow to the left of its text, and a negative y-offset will place the shadow above the text.

Notes

This is the mechanism by which authors may add "drop shadows" to their text without having to resort to graphics. The CSS specification does not say how, or even whether, shadows should be blended with their backgrounds, nor exactly how the blur should be calculated.

A shadow does not affect the size of the element's box, and may in fact extend beyond the element. The shadows are considered a part of their element's stacking context (see `z-index` for more details), and so may overlap other elements. The specification does not say how multiple shadows on the same element should be stacked or blended.

By specifying no offset and a blur radius for an element, it is possible to provide a "glow" effect to the element's text. Caution should be used, however, since many such effects involve setting the text color close to the background color, which will make the element very difficult to read in a user agent which does not support `text-shadow`. As of this writing, that was all of them, so authors are urged to use this property with caution.

Examples

```
h1 {text-shadow: 0.5em 0.4em 2px gray;}
p.raise {text-shadow: 1px 1px;}
```

4

```
div.crazy {text-shadow: 10px 1.2em 3px purple, -1in 23px 0 magenta,
    0 2em 1em maroon, 3ex -2cm 5mm yellow;}
```

Related Properties
None

text-transform

`text-transform` changes the capitalization of text within an element, or else directs the user agent to leave the capitalization "as is."

Summary

Value Syntax
capitalize | uppercase | lowercase | none | inherit

Initial Value
none

Percentages
n/a

Inherited
yes

Applies to
all elements

Media Groups
visual

Values

capitalize
The first letter of each word in the element's text should be capitalized. The CSS specification does not say what a "word" is, and in fact the definition of what constitutes a word is likely to be different from language to language. The usual working definition of a word is any sequence of characters which is surrounded by whitespace, but this cannot be guaranteed.

uppercase
All of the characters in the element's text should be uppercase (capital letters).

lowercase
All of the characters in the element's text should be lowercase.

none
The capitalization of the element's text should not be altered.

Notes

Although `text-transform` is inherited, it does not necessarily force the capitalization of the first letter in a descendent element. If a portion of a word is enclosed within an element, but there is no whitespace which separates this element from the text that surrounds it, then the string of letters is considered to be a single "word" and only the first letter in that word should be capitalized. Consider the following markup:

```
<em style="text-transform: capitalize;">
   supercali<strong>fragilistic</strong>expialidocious</em>
```

Only the first "S" would be capitalized, and the "f" at the beginning of the STRONG element would not.

Examples

```
*.shout {text-transform: uppercase;}
p.cummings {text-transform: lowercase;}
h1.title {text-transform: capitalize;}
```

Related Properties
None

top

`top` defines an offset of the top edge of an absolutely positioned element from the top edge of its positioning context, or the vertical distance which a relatively positioned element will be displaced.

Summary

Value Syntax
`<length> | <percentage> | auto | inherit`

Initial Value
`auto`

Percentages
refer to height of containing block

Inherited
no

Applies to
positioned elements

Media Groups
visual

Values

<length>
A fixed distance from the top of the positioning context.

<percentage>
Some percentage of the height of the positioning context, assuming that the height of the context has been set explicitly. If not, then a percentage value for `top` is treated as though it were `auto`. In practice, this means that percentage values for `top` set on relatively positioned elements will be ignored.

auto
The actual distance which results will depend on a number of factors. These factors are the dimensions of vertical measure for an absolutely positioned element (see the notes section). If the element has been relatively positioned, then `auto` has no apparent effect.

Notes

In the case of an absolutely positioned element, the vertical dimensions of the element must add up to the height of the positioning context. Setting `top` to `auto` may force other vertical dimensions which are also set to `auto` to be reset to 0. See the section on positioning calculations in Chapter 1 for more information.

In the case of relatively positioned elements, `top` defines a vertical offset from the place where the relatively positioned element would ordinarily have appeared. Positive values for `top` will offset the element upward, and negative values will move it downward. If both `bottom` and `top` are set to explicit values, then the value for `top` will be discarded in favor of `bottom`.

Examples

```
div.sidebar {position: absolute; width: 15em; margin: 0; padding: 0;
   height: auto; top: 25%;}
sub {vertical-align: baseline; position: relative; top: 0.5em;}
```

Related Properties
bottom, height, left, position, right

unicode-bidi

unicode-bidi influences the layout of text in bidirectional-text situations.

Summary

Value Syntax
normal | embed | bidi-override | inherit

Initial Value
normal

Percentages
n/a

Inherited
no

Applies to
all elements, but see notes

Media Groups
visual

Values

normal
Prevents the element from opening a new level of Unicode bidirectional embedding.

embed
Causes the element to open a new level of Unicode bidirectional embedding, assuming the element is inline-level. The direction of the new embedding level is taken from the value of the property direction for the element, and reordering within the element is implicit. For direction: ltr, this will have the effect of beginning the element with a Unicode LRE (U+202A); for direction: rtl, the element begins with a Unicode RLE (U+202B). In either case, the element will be closed with a Unicode PDF (U+202C).

bidi-override

Causes an override of reordering mechanisms within the element, assuming the element is inline-level or is a block-level element that contains only inline elements. In other words, glyphs within the element are strictly ordered in the direction specified by the property `direction`, and implicit ordering is ignored. For `direction: ltr`, this will have the effect of opening the element with a Unicode LRO (U+202D); for `direction: rtl`, the element begins with a Unicode ROL (U+202E). In either case, the element will be closed with a Unicode PDF (U+202C).

Notes

To quote the CSS2 specification: "The final order of the characters in each block-level element is the same as if the bidi control codes had been added as described..., markup had been stripped, and the resulting character sequence had been passed to an implementation of the Unicode bidirectional algorithm for plain text that produced the same line-breaks as the styled text. In this process, no-textual entities such as images are treated as neutral characters, unless their `unicode-bidi` property has a value other than `normal`, in which case they are treated as strong characters in the `direction` specified for the element." Authors who wish to understand this process in more detail should consult the Unicode specification, as an explanation of its workings is (far) beyond the scope of this book.

Examples

```
*:lang(en) {direction: ltr; unicode-bidi: embed;}
```

Related Properties

`direction`

vertical-align

`vertical-align` determines the alignment of text within a line, or within a table cell.

Summary

Value Syntax

baseline | sub | super | top | text-top | middle | bottom | text-bottom | <percentage> | <length> | inherit

Initial Value

baseline

Percentages

refer to the value of `line-height` for the element itself

Inherited

no

Applies to

inline-level elements and elements with a `display` of `table-cell`

Media Groups

visual

Values

baseline

The baseline of the element is aligned with the baseline of the parent element. If either element doesn't have a baseline, then align the bottom of the element box with the bottom of the parent element's box.

sub

The baseline of the element is lowered to the point appropriate for subscripted text. The CSS specification does not say what that point should be. Note that the value of `font-size` for the element is not altered by this value.

super

The baseline of the element is raised to the point appropriate for superscripted text. The CSS specification does not say what that point should be. Note that the value of `font-size` for the element is not altered by this value.

top

The top of the element's box is aligned with the top of the line box, in the context of inline content, or with the top of the table cell in the context of tables.

text-top

The top of the element's box is aligned with the top of the highest inline box in the line.

middle

The baseline of the element is aligned with the point defined by the baseline of the parent element plus half the x-height of the parent element's font, in the context of inline content. The middle of the element should be aligned with the middle of the table cell in the context of tables.

bottom
The bottom of the element's box is aligned with the bottom of the line box, in the context of inline content, or with the bottom of the table cell in the context of tables.

text-bottom
The bottom of the element's box is aligned with the bottom of the lowest inline box in the line.

<percentage>
The baseline of the element is raised or lowered by the given percentage of the value for the property `line-height`. Thus, a `vertical-align` value of `50%` on a line which has a `line-height` of `18px` will raise the baseline by 9 pixels. A percentage value of `0%` for this property has the same effect as the value `baseline`.

<length>
The baseline of the element is raised or lowered by the given length value. Negative length values are permitted for this property. A length value of `0` for this property has the same effect as the value `baseline`.

Notes
See the section on inline formatting in Chapter 1 for more details on the differences between line boxes, inline boxes, and the baseline.

Support for `vertical-align` is less than exemplary in current Web browsers. Only with the advent of browsers such as Internet Explorer 5 for Macintosh and Opera 4 have Web browsers truly supported the behavior described in the CSS specification. Older browsers may evidence unexpected behaviors, generally in the form of misaligning elements. In most cases, there is minimal impact on the layout (something which the author will tolerate), but attempts at extreme typographic effects may be thwarted by browser limitations.

Examples
```
sup {vertical-align: superscript; font-size: 80%;}
td div {vertical-align: middle;}
img.textdec {vertical-align: bottom;}
span.drop {vertical-align: text-bottom;}
```

Related Properties
```
line-height
```

visibility

`visibility` determines whether an element is invisible or not.

Summary

Value Syntax
`visible | hidden | collapse | inherit`

Initial Value
`inherit`

Percentages
n/a

Inherited
no

Applies to
all elements

Media Groups
visual

Values

visible
The element is visible.

hidden
The element is invisible (i.e., completely transparent). The element still exists, so it still affects the document's layout. The visual effect will be that of a blank spot exactly the same size that the visible element would occupy, including any borders or margins.

collapse
This value causes columns, rows, columns groups, and row groups to be removed from the document, but still affects the layout of the table. Thus, any cells within those rows will affect the widths of columns in the visible portion of the table.

Notes

The descendant elements of an invisible element may be made visible by setting them to `visibility: visible`.

This property is often used in "dynamic pages" to accomplish such effects as pop-up menus.

Examples

```
p.glass {visibility: hidden;}
tr.stow {visibility: collapse;}
```

Related Properties

```
display
```

white-space

`white-space` is used to alter the user agent's handling of whitespace in an element.

Summary

Value Syntax
```
normal | pre | nowrap | inherit
```

Initial Value
```
normal
```

Percentages
n/a

Inherited
yes

Applies to
block-level elements

Media Groups
visual

Values

normal
Any sequence of whitespaces within the element is converted to a single space. This is familiar behavior from traditional Web browsers.

pre
All whitespace in the element is honored, including multiple spaces and carriage returns. Word wrapping is disabled, and lines are only broken at newline characters in the source, or \A sequence in generated content.

nowrap
Any sequence of whitespaces within the element is converted to a single space, but word wrapping is disabled. Line breaks in the source are ignored, and only the \A sequence in generated content will start a new line of text.

Notes
Although the value nowrap is fairly well supported in modern browsers, pre is not.

Examples
```
div.poem {white-space: pre;}
p {white-space: normal;}
td.single {white-space: nowrap;}
```

Related Properties
None.

width

width sets the width of an element's content area.

Summary

Value Syntax
<length> | <percentage> | auto | inherit

Initial Value
auto

Percentages
refer to width of containing block

Inherited
no

Applies to
all elements except non-replaced inline elements, table rows, and row groups

Media Groups
visual

Values

<length>
Any length unit. Negative length values are not permitted for this property.

<percentage>
The width is calculated with respect to the width of the element's containing block, assuming that the containing block's width has been explicitly set. If not, then a percentage value is treated as `auto`.

auto
The result of this value depends on a number of factors. In the normal document flow, `auto` will be treated as `100%`, assuming that there are no margins, borders, or padding set on the element. For floated elements, the value `auto` will tend toward a width `0`. In positioned elements, it may have the same effect, or it may be overridden due to constraints introduced using properties such as `left` and `right`. See the section on positioning rules in Chapter 1 for more details.

Notes

If the width of a replaced element (e.g., an image) is set to a length unit, and no height is set, then the image will be scaled so that its width matches the declared value, and the height is altered by the same proportion. For example, an image 100 pixels tall and 50 pixels wide is set to `width: 200px`; thus its height will be increased to 100 pixels. Setting the width of a replaced element to a percentage will operate as described above, and make the width of the element some percentage of the width of its containing block. It is not possible to reduce an element to half its intrinsic size through a percentage value, for example.

Examples
```
div.aside {width: 25%;}
img.photo {width: 250px;}
```

Related Properties
`height`, `max-width`, `min-width`

word-spacing

`word-spacing` modifies the amount of space placed between words.

Summary

Value Syntax
normal | <length> | inherit

Initial Value
normal

Percentages
n/a

Inherited
yes

Applies to
all elements

Media Groups
visual

Values

normal
The default spacing between words is not changed. In practice, this is equivalent to setting the value to 0.

<length>
This will add to the spacing between words—the greater the length, the more space will be seen between words. Negative values are permitted, and will cause words to bunch together, to the point of potentially overwriting one another or even appearing to write the words "backwards." The length given will modify the amount of space already between words, which means that there is usually a minimum of a single space from which the modification occurs.

Notes

In fully justified text (see text-align), the space between words may be programmatically altered in order to create the effect of full justification.

In order to preserve the relative spacing between words for descendant elements, authors are encouraged to use em length units.

Examples
```
em {letter-spacing: 1px;}
h1.wider {letter-spacing: 0.5em;}
```

```
p.scrunched {letter-spacing: -0.5ex;}
table {letter-spacing: normal;}
```

Related Properties
letter-spacing, text-align

z-index

z-index sets the stacking level of an element.

Summary

Value Syntax
auto | <integer> | inherit

Initial Value
auto

Percentages
n/a

Inherited
no

Applies to
positioned elements

Media Groups
visual

Values

auto
The stack level of the element is the same as that of its parent element. Furthermore, the element does not generate a new stacking context.

<integer>
The stack level of the element is set to the given value, and it establishes a new stacking context for any descendant elements. The stack level of the element in its newly created stacking context is 0. The higher an element's z-index value, the "closer" it is to the reader. Negative values are permitted for this property. In theory, any arbitrarily large number may be declared, but there may be implementation-specific limits.

Notes

The *stack level* of an element is simply a numeric designation of its position on the *z-axis*. This axis is imagined as a line extending out of the canvas as well as behind it, although no element may ever be placed "behind" the canvas. An element is placed on the z-axis, and also given its stack level, using the property z-index. For example, elements A and B are given z-index values of 2 and 1044, respectively. In any situation where A and B overlap due to their positioning, then all of B will be visible, whereas part of A will appear to be "behind" B.

If an element generates a *stacking context*, then all of its descendant elements are placed on the z-axis as a group. Thus, no matter what values are assigned to descendants of element B, they will be placed "in front" of element A and its descendants. For those familiar with vector graphics programs such as Adobe Illustrator, a stacking context is basically equivalent to a layer on which many shapes may be placed. The shapes in each level will have a stacking order comparable to each other, but all of them will be "in front" of the layer below their layer.

The usual way to envision this is to add another stacking number for each context in which an element exists. For example, assume that element B, still with a z-index value of 1044, has a descendant element B2 with a z-index value of -40. Element A (z-index of 2) has a descendant element A2 with a z-index of 5000. If A2 and B2 overlap, B2 will still be "in front" of A2. Their z-index values can be thought of like this: A2, 2,5000; B2, 1044,-40. In summary, the four elements in question would be sorted this way:

```
A    2
A2   2,5000
B2   1044,-40
B    1044
```

Note that elements with a z-index of auto are effectively assigned places along the z-axis by the user agent, but there is no defined behavior for such a case. A user agent could decide to stack such elements in the order they are rendered, with the earliest elements in the document being the furthest away from the user. Of course, a user agent could do just the opposite, deciding that the last elements in a document will be furthest away from the user on the theory that the first elements contain the most important information. There is no way to guarantee any particular behavior.

Examples

```
div.sidebar {position: fixed; height: 100%; width: 20%; left: 0;
    z-index: 10;}
em#drop {position: relative; top: 14px; z-index: -66;}
```

Related Properties

```
position
```

Chapter 5
Paged Media Styles

One of the areas in which CSS2 improves greatly over CSS1 is in its addition of rules for handling paged media. This is usually assumed to refer to material such as printouts of a document, but it can also refer to specialized devices which display information a page at a time, as well as to "print previews" on a computer screen, and more. A good example is the default display of PDF files, which are usually presented a page at a time.

In creating a model for paged media, CSS takes the general idea of the box model and extends it to create the *page box*. This is the term used to refer to the area in which content is drawn on a given piece of the display medium (e.g., a piece of paper in a printout). The area in which a page box is drawn is referred to as a *sheet*. This term is used mostly to avoid the confusion which using the term "page" would invoke. In CSS2, all page boxes are rectangular, although they may not necessarily be the same size as the sheets on which they are drawn.

Because the page box is drawn from the general box model in CSS2, authors are able to set margins and dimensions for a page box, just as they would with an ordinary element box (however, padding and borders cannot be set on page boxes in CSS2). All this is done using the `@page` directive, which is explained later in the chapter.

As of CSS2, the specification does not contain properties to automatically generate running heads or footers, place page numbers, and other advanced page-layout features. These features are expected to appear in a future version of CSS. CSS2 does allow authors to simulate these features with the property `display` (see Chapter 4), although the methods are a bit clumsy.

General Paged-Media Rules

There are some concepts which should be understood before attempting to write paged-media styles. These include page-breaking and content-clipping rules.

Page-Breaking Rules

A good portion of the paged media rules are devoted to affecting the placement of page breaks. In order to keep these as clear as possible, CSS defines a number of rules related to "allowed" page breaks. This section will review these rules in order to make the properties which follow easier to understand.

In general, CSS recommends the use of some general heuristics to determine how page breaks should be placed.

- Break pages as few times as possible.
- Attempt to make all page boxes appear to be about the same height.
- Avoid page breaks inside block boxes which have borders.
- Avoid page breaks inside tables.
- Avoid page breaks inside floated elements.

The specification comes right out and admits that these rules may contradict each other in some circumstances. It also avoids making them actual requirements; thus, user agents are free to place page breaks as many or as few times as possible, and to use or ignore any or all of the preceding rules.

However, there are some rules which user agents may not ignore. First are the two basic rules which define where page breaks may actually occur.

- Page breaks may occur in the vertical margins between block boxes. If a page break occurs between two block boxes, then the adjacent margins (the bottom margin of the preceding element and the top margin of the following elements) are set to 0.
- Page breaks may occur between the line boxes of a block box.

There is more to the story than that, as it happens. There are five rules which govern the placement of page breaks.

1. A page break may only be placed between block boxes if the values of `page-break-after` and `page-break-before` for the two affected elements will allow it. This is the case if the value of at least one of the elements is `always`, `left`, or `right`; or if the values for both elements is `auto`.

2. If the values of `page-break-after` and `page-break-before` for two adjacent elements is `auto`, and the nearest common ancestor to the two elements has a `page-break-inside` value of `avoid`, then do not place a page break between the elements.

3. A page break may be placed between two line boxes in a block box only if the number of line boxes between the line box and the start of the block box is greater than or equal to the value of `orphans` for the element. Similarly, a page break may be placed between two line boxes only if the number of line boxes between the line box and the end of the block box is greater than or equal to the value of `widows` for the element.

4. A page break may be placed between two line boxes of an element only when the value of `page-break-inside` for the element is `auto`.

5. A page break must be placed between two block boxes if the value of `page-break-before` (for the preceding element) or `page-break-after` (for the following element) is `always`, `left`, or `right`.

In situations where the rules do not allow for a line break, then rules 1 and 3 are ignored in order to allow more flexibility. If there is still no valid place for a line break to appear, then rules 2 and 4 are also ignored. In other words, all bets are off. At this point, the user agent will likely perform some form of straightforward clipping operation to split the page, but other behaviors may be used. Rule 5 always takes effect, no matter the circumstance.

Now that we've explored the circumstances in which a page break *may* be placed, let's look at the two rules which describe when a page break *must* be placed.

1. A page break must be placed between two block boxes if the value of `page` is different for the two blocks.

2. A page break must be placed between two block boxes if the value of `page` for the last line box in the preceding element is

different than the value of `page` for the first line box of the following element.

Finally, page breaks cannot be placed inside absolutely positioned elements.

Content-Clipping Rules

If content somehow ends up beyond the confines of the page box—for example, if it is an especially wide image, or an element which has been positioned too far to one side or another—then the browser must choose some mechanism to cope with the situation. As with the basic page-breaking rules, there are a few suggestions.

- Content should be permitted to "bleed" beyond the edges of the page box. In other words, user agents should render content which is outside the page box so long as there is room to do so.

- Although it may be necessary to generate blank pages to honor the values `left` and `right` for the page-break rules, generation of an excessive number of empty page boxes should be avoided.

- If an element is positioned outside the page box to the extent that no part of it will be rendered, then the user agent may choose its own method of handling it. It may discard the element, for example, or place it at the end of the document.

Since none of these behaviors are requirements, authors cannot rely on any particular behavior to happen in all user agents. For this reason, the CSS specification also recommends that authors not create rules to place elements in odd positions simply to avoid rendering them. If an element should not be rendered in paged media, then it can be suppressed using `display: none` or made invisible with `visibility: hidden`.

Reference

@page

`@page` is used to define the page context for a given page box.

Summary

Syntax
`@page <page selector>?<page pseudo-class>? {<page context>}`

Media Groups
`paged`

Components

<page selector>
Any legal string value may be used to define the page selector. For example, a page selector meant to describe one page of a greeting card could be called `card`, `greeting-card`, or anything else which has meaning for the author. Similarly, a page selector for handheld devices could be `palm-screen` or `hand-screen`. The page selector can then be utilized by way of the property `page`.

<page pseudo-class>
This can be any of the page pseudo-classes `:first`, `:left`, and `:right` (see the upcoming descriptions). These pseudo-classes must follow the page selector with no intervening space.

<page context>
The block of CSS rules which describe the page box.

Description
The page context is especially notable for the restrictions which are imposed upon it and the way in which it changes the behavior of a few visual properties.

First of all, a page box cannot be given padding or borders—only margins—so these properties will have no effect in a page context. (The CSS2 specification expressly states that this may change in the future.) Second (and more important), a page context has no concept of fonts, which means that `em` and `ex` units cannot be used to describe the size of a page box or its margins. All such dimensions must be declared with an absolute-length unit such as `in` or `cm`, or the relative-size length unit `px` (pixels). Note, however, that the mapping of pixels to a paged medium is not defined and cannot be guaranteed. It is possible that a laser printer, for example, would interpret a length of `600px` as 600 dots. At a resolution of 1200 dots per inch or more, this would be a very small length. For this reason, the use of pixels in paged media is strongly discouraged.

One property whose behavior changes in a paged-medium context is `position`. When an element is set to `position: fixed`, it will appear in the same position on every page. This can be useful for creating effects such as running heads and footers. If this is done, care must be taken to make sure that the fixed-position element does not overlap other content on the page. This could be accomplished by increasing the margins on the page box on the appropriate side.

A page context may be established for any element, including the BODY element in HTML. If an element has a different page context from the element which precedes it, then a page break should be inserted between them. See the section on page later in this chapter for more details.

Examples

```
@page sideways {size: landscape; margin: 0.75in;}
@page {size: 8.5in 11in; marks: cross; margin: 1in;}
@page legal:first {size: 8.5in 14in; margin: 0.66in; margin-top: 3in;}
```

Related Properties

page

:first

The pseudo-class :first is used to style the first page of a document.

Summary

Syntax
```
@page <page selector>?:first {<page context>}
```

Media Groups
paged

Description

By using :first, the author can set special styles for the first page of a document which will not carry over to other pages. This could be an increased top margin, for example, or a portrait orientation when the rest of the document is in landscape.

Examples

```
@page :first {size: portrait; margin-top: 2.5in;}
@page rotate:first {size: landscape; margin-bottom: 10mm;}
```

:left

The pseudo-class :left is used to style the left pages of a document.

Summary

Syntax
@page <page selector>?:left {<page context>}

Media Groups
paged

Description

This pseudo-class allows authors to define styles for pages which are on the left in double-sided printing. For example, in one common paged-media layout format, the right margin (which will be toward the "inside" of a two-page layout) of left-side pages should be larger to account for binding, while the left (or "outer") margin should be equivalent to the top and bottom margins. This can be accomplished with simple margin rules for all :left pages.

Examples

```
@page :left {margin-right: 1.25in; margin-left: 1in;
    margin-top: 1in; margin-bottom: 1in;}
```

:right

The pseudo-class :right is used to style the right pages of a document.

Summary

Syntax
@page <page selector>?:right {<page context>}

Media Groups
paged

Description

This pseudo-class allows authors to define styles for pages which are on the right in double-sided printing, such as increasing the margin width for the left ("inside") margin to account for binding (see the previous description of :left for details). This can be accomplished with simple margin rules for all :right pages.

Examples
```
@page :right {margin-left: 1.25in; margin-right: 1in;
    margin-top: 1in; margin-bottom: 1in;}
```

marks

marks specifies the appearance and type of cropping marks which are placed on each page.

Summary
Value Syntax
[crop || cross] | none | inherit

Initial Value
none

Percentages
n/a

Inherited
n/a

Applies to
page context

Media Groups
visual, paged

Values

crop
Directs that crop marks be placed on the page. These marks are used by printers to determine where a page should be trimmed.

cross
Causes the user agent to add cross marks to the page. These marks are used to align sheets during the printing process.

none
No marks should be placed on the page.

Notes

The marks which are invoked with this property are placed just outside the page box, the size of which is determined by the property size.

The placement, size, and appearance of the marks is entirely under the control of the user agent, and cannot be affected through CSS.

Examples

```
@page proof {marks: cross crop; margin: 1.5em; size: auto;}
@page {marks: none;}
```

Related Properties

size

orphans

orphans sets the minimum number of lines in an element that must appear at the bottom of a page.

Summary

Value Syntax
<integer> | inherit

Initial Value
2

Percentages
n/a

Inherited
yes

Applies to
block-level elements

Media Groups
visual, paged

Values

<integer>
The number given sets the minimum number of lines permitted at the bottom of a page. The value of orphans can affect the

page-breaking for a given page, effectively moving the "break point" up or down depending on the circumstances. For example, assume an element which starts one line before the bottom of the page box. If the value of `orphans` is 2, then the page break will be placed before the element, and it will start on the next page. This will have the side effect of increasing the "blank space" at the bottom of the page.

Notes

The value of `orphans` will be invoked for a given element only if that element should have a page break within it. In other words, an element which started just before the end of a page and which carries over to the next page will use its `orphans` value. Any element which fits onto a single page in its entirety can have a value for `orphans`, but will not use it.

Setting the value of `orphans` sufficiently high can lead to strange effects. If you set `orphans` to 20 for all elements in a document, then any element which is longer than 20 lines and starts less than 20 lines before the bottom of the page will be shifted to the next page.

Examples

```
p {orphans: 3;}
ol {orphans: 5;}
```

Related Properties

`page-break-after`, `page-break-before`, `page-break-inside`, `widows`

page

`page` is used to invoke a page selector which has been previously defined using `@page`.

Summary

Value Syntax
`<page selector> | auto`

Initial Value
`auto`

Percentages
n/a

Inherited
yes

Applies to
block-level elements

Media Groups
visual, paged

Values

<page selector>
Any previously defined page selector. See the section on @page earlier in the chapter for more details.

auto
The user agent should format the page according to its defaults.

Notes

As a property, page can have no apparent effect on page layout without a previously defined page selector to use. It is useful, however, in that a page selector can be defined for a particular page layout, and then that layout can be assigned to individual elements. For example, suppose that you have a type of table which needs to be printed in landscape mode. By assigning a consistent class to these tables (e.g., <table class="chart">), you can then use page to assign a landscape-oriented page context to these elements. Since their page context will differ from surrounding elements, these tables will appear on their own pages, with page breaks being inserted before and after the landscape tables.

If you wish to apply a consistent page context to the entire document, you can create a page selector and then select the BODY element with a page rule set to that page selector.

Examples
```
@page proof {marks: cross crop; margin: 1.5em; size: auto;}
body.rough-draft {page: proof;}
@page rotate {size: landscape;}
table.chart {page: rotate;}
```

Related Properties
@page

page-break-after

`page-break-after` indicates whether (and how many) page breaks should be allowed after an element's box.

Summary

Value Syntax
auto | always | avoid | left | right | inherit

Initial Value
auto

Percentages
n/a

Inherited
no

Applies to
block-level elements

Media Groups
visual, paged

Values

auto
Page breaks should be neither forced nor prevented after the element's box.

always
A page break should be forced after this element's box.

avoid
No page break should be placed after the element's box if at all possible. This does not guarantee the lack of a page break after the element.

left
Force one or two page breaks after the element's box, such that the next page on which an element is printed will be a left-hand page.

right
Force one or two page breaks after the element's box, such that the next page on which an element is printed will be a right-hand page.

Notes

The value of this property is not the sole factor in determining whether a page break should follow the element. This decision will also be affected by the value of `page-break-before` for a following element, and the value of `page-break-inside` for any ancestor elements.

Examples

```
h1 {page-break-after: avoid;}
div.summary {page-break-after: always;}
```

Related Properties

`orphans`, `page-break-before`, `page-break-inside`, `widows`

page-break-before

`page-break-before` indicates whether (and how many) page breaks should be allowed before an element's box.

Summary

Value Syntax
auto | always | avoid | left | right | inherit

Initial Value
auto

Percentages
n/a

Inherited
no

Applies to
block-level elements

Media Groups
visual, paged

Values

auto
Page breaks should be neither forced nor prevented before the element's box.

always
A page break should be forced before the element's box.

avoid
No page break should be placed before the element's box, if at all possible. This does not guarantee the lack of a page break before the element.

left
Force one or two page breaks before the element's box, such that the page on which the element is printed will be a left-hand page.

right
Force one or two page breaks before the element's box, such that the page on which the element is printed will be a right-hand page.

Notes
The value of this property is not the sole factor in determining whether a page break should follow the element. This decision will also be affected by the value of `page-break-after` for a preceding element, and the value of `page-break-inside` for any ancestor elements.

Examples
```
h1 {page-break-before: right;}
table {page-break-before: always;}
```

Related Properties
`orphans`, `page-break-after`, `page-break-inside`, `widows`

page-break-inside

`page-break-inside` indicates whether page breaks should be allowed within an element's box.

Summary

Value Syntax
`avoid | auto | inherit`

Initial Value
`auto`

Percentages
n/a

Inherited
yes

Applies to
block-level elements

Media Groups
visual, paged

Values

avoid
No page break should be placed inside the element's box if at all possible. This is not a guarantee, as the element may be too large to fit on a single page.

auto
Page breaks should be neither forced nor prevented inside the element's box.

Notes

The value of this property is not the sole factor in determining whether a page break should follow the element. This decision will also be affected by the values of `page-break-before` and `page-break-after` for any descendant elements. For example, if a `DIV` is set to `page-break-inside: avoid`, but one of its descendant elements has been set to `page-break-before: always`, then there will be a page break inside the `DIV`.

Examples

```
ul, ol {page-break-inside: avoid;}
table {page-break-inside: avoid;}
p {page-break-inside: auto;}
```

Related Properties

`orphans`, `page-break-after`, `page-break-before`, `widows`

size

`size` specifies the size and orientation of a page box.

Summary

Value Syntax
`<length>{1,2} | auto | portrait | landscape | inherit`

Initial Value
auto

Percentages
n/a

Inherited
n/a

Applies to
page context

Media Groups
visual, paged

Values

<length>
Sets the physical size of the page box. If only one length value is given, it sets both the height and width of the page box. If two length values are given, the first is the width and the second the height of the page box.

auto
The page box is sized to fit the display medium. For example, if the print page is 8.5 inches by 11 inches, then page: auto will result in a page box of that size.

portrait
Sets the page box to the same size as the display sheet, but the longer measure is forced to be the vertical axis. As an example, if the sheet is 5 inches tall by 10 inches wide, a setting of size: portrait will force the user agent to make the page box 10 inches tall by 5 inches wide. On the other hand, an 8.5 inch by 11 inch sheet will result in a page box which is 8.5 inches wide by 11 inches tall.

landscape
Sets the page box to the same size as the display sheet, but the longer measure is forced to be the horizontal axis. As an example, if the sheet is 5 inches tall by 10 inches wide, a setting of size: landscape will force the user agent to make the page box 5 inches tall by 10 inches wide. On the other hand, an 8.5 inch by 11 inch sheet will result in a page box which is 11 inches wide by 8.5 inches tall.

Notes

If the page box which results from the values of size will not fit on the actual sheet, then the CSS specification offers two possible fallbacks. First is to rotate the page box 90 degrees, assuming this will allow the page box to fit onto a sheet. If this is not the case, then the user agent may scale the page box to fit on the sheet.

It is also left to user agents to decide where the page box will actually be placed on the sheet, although the CSS specification recommends that it be centered within the sheet.

Examples

```
@page legal {size: 8.5in 14in;}
@page {size: landscape;}
```

Related Properties

`@page`

widows

`widows` sets the minimum number of lines in an element that must appear at the top of a page.

Summary

Value Syntax
`<integer>` | `inherit`

Initial Value
2

Percentages
n/a

Inherited
yes

Applies to
block-level elements

Media Groups
visual, paged

Values

<integer>

The number given sets the minimum number of lines permitted at the top of a page. The value of `widows` can affect the page-breaking for a given page, effectively moving the "break point" up or down depending on the circumstances. For example, assume an element which should end one line after the top of the page box. If the value of `widows` is 2, then the page break will be placed before the element, and it will start on the current page. This will have the side effect of increasing the "blank space" at the bottom of the previous page.

Notes

The value of `widows` will be invoked for a given element only if that element should have a page break within it. In other words, an element which started just before the end of a page and which carries over to the next page will use its `widows` value. Any element which fits onto a single page in its entirety can have a value for `widows`, but will not use it.

Setting the value of `widows` sufficiently high can lead to strange effects. If you set `widows` to 20 for all elements in a document, then any element which ends less than 20 lines after the top of the page will be shifted in its entirety onto the page, thereby removing it from the previous page.

Examples

```
div.aside {widows: 2;}
ul {widows: 6;}
```

Related Properties

orphans, page-break-after, page-break-before,
page-break-inside

Chapter 6
Aural Media Styles

In addition to the visual and paged media, CSS also provides properties to support aural (audio) media. Using these properties, it is theoretically possible to create audio styles nearly as rich as the visual styles permitted by the rest of the specification. Besides enriching the Web for users who are blind or otherwise visually impaired, aural styles could also be useful for automobile drivers who want to have Web pages read to them by a dashboard browser, just to pick one example.

As of this writing, there is very little deployed support for aural styles, and what support does exist can be found in niche products which exist to serve the visually impaired community. None of the popular visual browsers, such as Netscape Navigator or Microsoft Internet Explorer, includes any support for aural styles.

Reference

azimuth

`azimuth` describes the position of a sound source along the horizontal axis of the listener's environment.

Summary

Value Syntax
```
<angle> | [[ left-side | far-left | left |
center-left | center | center-right | right |
far-right | right-side ] || behind ] | leftwards |
rightwards | inherit
```

Initial Value
center

Percentages
n/a

Inherited
yes

Applies to
all elements

Media Groups
aural

Values

<angle>

Any angle value which corresponds to the range 0deg – 360deg.
An angle value of 0deg corresponds to a point directly in front of
the listener, whereas 90deg corresponds to a point directly to the
right, 180deg a point directly behind, and 270deg directly to the
left of the listener. Negative angle values are also permitted, so
-90deg is equivalent to 270deg.

left-side

Equivalent to 270deg (-90deg). When combined with behind,
the sound's position is the same.

far-left

Equivalent to 300deg (-60deg). When combined with behind,
the sound's position is equivalent to 240deg.

left

Equivalent to 320deg (-40deg). When combined with behind,
the sound's position is equivalent to 220deg.

center-left

Equivalent to 340deg (-20deg). When combined with behind,
the sound's position is equivalent to 200deg.

center

Equivalent to 0deg. When combined with behind, the sound's
position is equivalent to 180deg.

center-right

Equivalent to 20deg. When combined with behind, the sound's
position is equivalent to 160deg.

right

Equivalent to 40deg. When combined with behind, the sound's
position is equivalent to 140deg.

far-right
Equivalent to `60deg`. When combined with `behind`, the sound's position is equivalent to `120deg`.

right-side
Equivalent to `90deg`. When combined with `behind`, the sound's position is the same.

leftwards
Causes the audio source to be shifted by 20 degrees (in 360-degree space) to the left. In fact, `leftwards` causes a shift in a counterclockwise direction. Thus, if the sound source is initially at the `180deg` position (directly behind the listener), then `leftwards` would actually cause the source to be shifted to `160deg`, or 20 degrees counterclockwise, which will sound to the listener like a rightward movement.

rightwards
Causes the audio source to be shifted by 20 degrees (in 360-degree space) to the right. In fact, `rightwards` causes a shift in a clockwise direction. Thus, if the sound source is initially at the `180deg` position (directly behind the listener), then `rightwards` would actually cause the source to be shifted to `200deg`, or 20 degrees clockwise, which will sound to the listener like a leftward movement.

Notes
If an aural device can produce spatial audio, but cannot place sounds behind the listener, then the device should convert the values between `90deg` and `270deg` into values in the `-90deg` to `90deg` range. The specification does not require a particular method of accomplishing this, but suggests an algorithm equivalent to the following:

> if `90deg` < x <=`270deg` then set x to `180deg` $-x$

This algorithm will "reflect" sounds from the rear hemisphere into the forward hemisphere. For example, a sound at `135deg` will be reflected to `45deg`, while a sound at `210deg` will be set to `-30deg` (equivalent to `330deg`).

Examples
```
a.external:link {azimuth: right-side;}
a:visited {azimuth: 180deg;}
```

Related Properties
elevation

cue

cue is a shorthand element for cue-before and cue-after.

Summary

Value Syntax
[<cue-before> || <cue-after>] | inherit

Initial Value
not defined for shorthand properties

Percentages
n/a

Inherited
no

Applies to
all elements

Media Groups
aural

Values

<cue-before>
See the entry for cue-before.

<cue-after>
See the entry for cue-after.

Notes
If two values are specified, the first corresponds to cue-before, and the second to cue-after. If only one value is given, it applies to both cue-before and cue-after.

Examples
```
h1 {cue: url(flourish.wav);}
a:link {cue: url(open.wav) url(close.wav);}
```

Related Properties
cue-before, cue-after, pause, pause-after, pause-before

cue-after

cue-after defines an auditory cue to be played immediately after the rendering of an element.

Summary

Value Syntax
<uri> | none | inherit

Initial Value
none

Percentages
n/a

Inherited
no

Applies to
all elements

Media Groups
aural

Values

<uri>
The user agent should use the sound resource defined by that URI as the audio cue. If the URI points to something other than an audio file, then it is to be ignored and the user agent should act as though cue-after had been set to none.

none
Setting cue-after to none means that no cue should be played.

Notes
cue-after can be used to play a "page turning" sound after each paragraph, sound a gong to mark the end of a hyperlink, or other audible cues. Note that this cue is rendered after any pauses declared using pause-after.

Examples

```
a:link {cue-after: url(close.wav);}
body {cue-after: url(the-end.wav);}
```

Related Properties

cue, cue-before, pause-after

cue-before

cue-before defines an auditory cue to be played immediately before the rendering of an element.

Summary

Value Syntax
<uri> | none | inherit

Initial Value
none

Percentages
n/a

Inherited
no

Applies to
all elements

Media Groups
aural

Values

<uri>
The user agent should use the sound resource defined by that URI as the audio cue. If the URI points to something other than an audio file, then it is to be ignored and the user agent should act as though cue-before had been set to none.

none
Setting cue-before to none means that no cue should be played.

Notes

cue-before can be used to play a "new section" sound before each heading, produce a "mouse-click" sound to mark the beginning of a hyperlink, or other audible cues. Note that this cue is rendered before any pauses declared using `pause-before`.

Examples
```
a:visited {cue-before: url(drag.wav);}
h3 {cue-before: url(ding.wav);}
```

Related Properties
`cue, cue-after, pause-before`

elevation

`elevation` describes the position of a sound source along the vertical axis of the listener's environment.

Summary

Value Syntax
`<angle>` | `above` | `level` | `below` | `higher` | `lower` | `inherit`

Initial Value
`level`

Percentages
n/a

Inherited
yes

Applies to
all elements

Media Groups
aural

Values

<angle>
Angle values are in the range `-90deg` to `90deg`. An angle value of `0deg` corresponds to a point which is level with the listener, whereas `90deg` corresponds to a point directly above, and `-90deg` directly below.

above
Equivalent to the value `90deg`.

level
Equivalent to the value 0deg.

below
Equivalent to the value -90deg.

higher
Causes the sound source to be shifted upwards by 10deg. Values beyond the range −90deg to 90deg are "clipped" to the edges of the range; thus, applying higher to a sound source with an elevation of 90deg will result in the value 90deg.

lower
Causes the sound source to be shifted downwards by 10deg. Values beyond the range −90deg to 90deg are "clipped" to the edges of the range; thus, applying lower to a sound source with an elevation of -90deg will result in the value -90deg.

Notes
By combining this property with azimuth, a sound's position in the "aural sphere" can be described.

Examples
```
h1 {elevation: above;}
h2 {elevation: 60deg;}
```

Related Properties
azimuth

pause

pause is a shorthand element for pause-before and pause-after.

Summary

Value Syntax
[[<time> | <percentage>]{1,2}] | inherit

Initial Value
UA dependent

Percentages
see descriptions of pause-before and pause-after

Inherited
no

Applies to
all elements

Media Groups
aural

Values

<time>
Any time value (e.g., 150ms); the pause will be the length of time specified.

<percentage>
The length of the pause is dictated by the value of speech-rate. For a speech-rate of 60 words per minute, which corresponds to one word per second, then a percentage is calculated with respect to one second. For a speech-rate of 120 words per minute, which yields a time per word of 500 milliseconds, then percentage would be calculated with respect to 500 milliseconds.

Notes
If two values are specified, the first corresponds to pause-before, and the second to pause-after. If only one value is given, it applies to both pause-before and pause-after.

Examples
```
a:link, a:visited {pause: 25%;}
h1 {pause: 2s 250ms;}
```

Related Properties
cue-before, cue-after, pause-before, pause-after, speech-rate

pause-after

pause-after defines the duration of a silent pause to be inserted after the content of an element.

Values
<time> | <percentage> | inherit

Initial Value
UA dependent

Percentages
see description under Values

Inherited
no

Applies to
all elements

Media Groups
aural

Values

<time>
Any time value (e.g., 300ms); the pause will be the length of time specified.

<percentage>
The length of the pause is dictated by the value of speech-rate. Thus, pause-after: 33% would yield 167ms if the speech rate is two words per second (120 words per minute), and 333ms if it's one word per second (60 words per minute).

Notes
The generated pause is observed before any cue-after content.

Examples
```
table {pause-after: 1500ms;}
li {pause-after: 50%;}
```

Related Properties
cue-after, pause, pause-before, speech-rate

pause-before

pause-before defines the duration of a silent pause to be inserted before the content of an element.

Summary

Value Syntax
<time> | <percentage> | inherit

Initial Value
UA dependent

Percentages
see description under Values

Inherited
no

Applies to
all elements

Media Groups
aural

6

Values

<time>
Any time value (e.g., 2s).

<percentage>
The length of the pause is dictated by the value of speech-rate.
Thus, pause-before: 50% would yield 250ms if the speech rate is
two words per second (120 words per minute), and 500ms if it's
one word per second (60 words per minute).

Notes

The generated pause is observed after any cue-before content.

Examples

```
h2, h3, h4 {pause-before: 200%;}
ol li {pause-before: 1s;}
```

Related Properties

cue-before, pause, pause-after, speech-rate

pitch

pitch specifies the average pitch of the speaking voice used to
render spoken text.

Summary

Value Syntax
<frequency> | x-low | low | medium | high | x-high | inherit

Initial Value
medium

Percentages
n/a

Inherited
yes

Applies to
all elements

Media Groups
aural

Values

<frequency>
A frequency value, which must be set in hertz (e.g., 140Hz), will define an absolute frequency to use as the pitch average.

x-low
While the corresponding absolute frequency will be different for every voice family, the result given by x-low must at a minimum be lower than the result derived from the keyword low.

low
While the corresponding absolute frequency will be different for every voice family, the result given by low must, at a minimum, be lower than the result derived from the keyword medium.

medium
While the corresponding absolute frequency will be different for every voice family, the result given by medium must, at a minimum, be higher than the result given by the keyword low, and lower than the result derived from the keyword high.

high
While the corresponding absolute frequency will be different for every voice family, the result given by high must, at a minimum, be higher than the result derived from the keyword medium.

x-high
While the corresponding absolute frequency will be different for every voice family, the result given by `x-high` must, at a minimum, be higher than the result derived from the keyword `high`.

Notes
The default average pitch will depend on the voice family; for example, the average male pitch is generally given as 120Hz, while the female average is in the area of 210Hz.

Examples
```
p.shriek {pitch: high;}
div.basso {pitch: x-low;}
body {pitch: 150Hz;}
```

Related Properties
`pitch-range, voice-family`

6

pitch-range

`pitch-range` defines the amount of variation permitted in the pitch of spoken text.

Summary

Value Syntax
`<number> | inherit`

Initial Value
`50`

Percentages
n/a

Inherited
yes

Applies to
all elements

Media Groups
aural

Values

<number>

The higher the value of `pitch-range`, the more "animated" a voice will seem, due to the changes in pitch used in speaking various words. A value of `0` will produce a voice with no pitch variation at all—in other words, a flat monotone. The value `50` is defined to correspond to "normal" inflection. Higher values will lead to a perception of more animation in the voice.

Notes

The number values are raw numbers, *not* frequency values. Thus, setting `pitch-range: 70` does *not* mean that the pitch can vary up to 70Hz. In fact, the pitch variation may be more or less than 70Hz, depending on the voice family and possibly a number of other unknown factors. The degree of pitch change for each numeric value of `pitch-range` is not defined by CSS.

Examples

```
body {pitch-range: 66;}
*.robot {pitch-range: 0;}
```

Related Properties

`pitch`, `voice-family`

play-during

`play-during` defines a sound to be played while rendering the element's content. This sound is also known as a "background sound."

Summary

Value Syntax
`<uri> mix? repeat? | auto | none | inherit`

Initial Value
`auto`

Percentages
n/a

Inherited
no

Applies to
all elements

Media Groups
aural

Values

<uri>
A single URI may be given, and it should resolve to a sound file. If it does not, then `play-during` is treated as though it had been set to `auto`.

mix
Causes the background sound of the element to be played, along with any background sound resulting from the value of `play-during` for any ancestor elements. If the value does not contain `mix`, then the element's background sound replaces the ancestor's background sound for the duration of the element's rendering. Once the element has been rendered, its background sound ceases and the ancestor's background sound resumes.

repeat
Causes the background sound to be repeated if it finishes before the element is fully rendered. If the value does not contain `repeat`, then the sound will only be played once. Any background sound which lasts longer than the rendering time for the element will be clipped once the element has been spoken, regardless of the presence or absence of `repeat`.

auto
Any sound being played for any ancestor elements will continue to be heard, but no background sound will be produced by the current element. If there is no sound associated with any ancestor elements, then no sound will be heard.

none
Causes complete background silence during the rendering of the element. No background sound is played for the element, and any background sounds associated with ancestor elements are also muted.

Notes

Due to the potential cacophony which could result from mixing several sounds together at once, authors are encouraged to use the keyword `mix` sparingly, and with a great deal of caution. This is especially true since CSS does not offer a way to synchronize sounds with each other.

Examples
```
h1 {play-during: url(ocean-waves.wav) mix repeat;}
a:link (play-during: none;)
```

Related Properties
none

richness

`richness` defines the degree to which a voice will "carry."

Summary

Value Syntax
<number> | inherit

Initial Value
50

Percentages
n/a

Inherited
yes

Applies to
all elements

Media Groups
aural

Values

<number>
The higher the numeric value, the more rich the voice and the further it will carry. A lower value will produce a voice which is soft and (to quote the specification) "mellifluous."

Notes
Richness is also known as the "brightness" of a voice.

Examples
```
*.chairman-kaga {richness: 80;}
div.aside {richness: 10;}
```

Related Properties
```
stress, voice-family
```

speak

`speak` defines the method by which an element's text should be aurally rendered, or if it should be rendered at all.

Summary

Value Syntax
```
normal | none | spell-out | inherit
```

Initial Value
```
normal
```

Percentages
n/a

Inherited
yes

Applies to
all elements

Media Groups
aural

Values

normal
Directs the user agent to speak the text using the pronunciation rules for that element and its children. These pronunciation rules will be language-dependent and are not given in CSS.

none
Prevents the element from being spoken. This is accomplished by skipping the element entirely. This is somewhat analogous to the visual style `display: none`, which suppresses rendering of an element and closes up the space it would ordinarily occupy. By skipping the element, the time taken to render it is effectively zero. In order to suppress audio rendering of an element but force the

browser to pause for the amount of time it normally would have taken to speak the element, see `volume`.

spell-out
Causes the user agent to speak the text one letter at a time, which is useful for speaking acronyms. For example, the `speak` value for an element containing the text "W3C" should probably be `spell-out`.

Notes

In a sense, `speak` is something like `display` for aural media, although `display` can still be used in aural stylesheets. In the case of `speak: none`, it is possible that descendant elements may override this value and thus be spoken. In order to ensure that an element and its descendants are not aurally rendered, use `display: none`.

Examples

```
acronym {speak: spell-out;}
*.hidden {speak: none;}
```

Related Properties

`speak-header`, `speaker-numeral`, `speak-punctuation`, `volume`

speak-header

`speak-header` is used to specify the audible repetition (or lack thereof) of table headers.

Summary

Value Syntax
once | always | inherit

Initial Value
once

Percentages
n/a

Inherited
yes

Applies to
elements that have table header information

Media Groups
aural

Values

once
Headers will only be read once; that is, they will be rendered when the user agent first renders the header cell.

always
The contents of the header will be spoken as the preface to every related cell in the table. Thus, for every cell in a column beneath the header "Sales Tax," the browser will speak the words "Sales Tax" before rendering the contents of the table cell. If a document language possesses no way to associate headers with other cells, then `speak-header: always` cannot be supported for documents in that language.

Notes

The correct execution of `speak-header` values is dependent on a document mechanism which associates cells with headers. For example, HTML 4.0 contains elements to describe columns and rows, as well as attribute-based association methods, and in addition describes a method of deducing header information from the structure of the table.

Examples
```
table {speak-header: once;}
th.urgent {speak-header: always;}
```

Related Properties
speak, speaker-numeral, speak-punctuation

speak-numeral

`speak-numeral` defines the method by which a number should be aurally rendered.

Summary

Value Syntax
digits | continuous | inherit

Initial Value
continuous

Percentages
n/a

Inherited
yes

Applies to
all elements

Media Groups
aural

Values

digits
The numeral is read one number at a time; e.g., "four one one."

continuous
The numeral is read in a language-dependent fashion; e.g., "four hundred eleven."

Notes
Language-dependent speaking systems are not within the scope of CSS, so each user agent may implement its own strategy for speaking numerals in a continuous fashion.

Examples
```
td.phone-no {speak-number: digits;}
td.price {speak-number: continuous;}
```

Related Properties
speak, speaker-header, speak-punctuation

speak-punctuation

speak-punctuation defines the method by which punctuation should be aurally rendered.

Summary

Value Syntax
code | none | inherit

Initial Value
none

Percentages
n/a

Inherited
yes

Applies to
all elements

Media Groups
aural

Values

code
Punctuation is spoken literally; e.g., "In closing comma I feel that..."

none
Punctuation is rendered as pauses of various lengths. The length of these pauses will be language-dependent.

Notes

Language-dependent speaking systems are not within the scope of CSS, so each user agent may implement its own strategy for "speaking" punctuation.

Examples

```
*.literal {speak-punctuation: code;}
body {speak-punctuation: none;}
```

Related Properties

speak, speak-header, speaker-numeral

speech-rate

speech-rate is used to declare the rate at which text is spoken.

Summary

Value Syntax
```
<number> | x-slow | slow | medium | fast | x-fast |
faster | slower | inherit
```

Initial Value
medium

Percentages
n/a

Inherited
yes

Applies to
all elements

Media Groups
aural

Values

<number>
Define the average number of words spoken per minute. Thus,
a value of 90 would set the user agent to read text at an average
of 90 words per minute.

x-slow
Equivalent to 80 words per minute.

slow
Equivalent to 120 words per minute.

medium
Equivalent to 180-200 words per minute. The exact number chosen
is user agent–dependent.

fast
Equivalent to 300 words per minute.

x-fast
Equivalent to 500 words per minute.

faster
Adds 40 words per minute to the current value of speech-rate.

slower
Subtracts 40 words per minute to the current value of speech-rate.

Notes

Note that the words-per-minute figures for the keywords are
normal for the English language. Although implementation
experience shows that other languages have different speaking

rates, these are not accommodated in the specification. Future revisions of CSS may or may not address this situation.

Examples

```
em {speech-rate: slower;}
div.legalese {speech-rate: fast;}
h1 {speech-rate: 90;}
```

Related Properties

`pause, pause-after, pause-before`

stress

`stress` specifies the amount of inflection which is used to speak stress markers in a language.

Summary

Value Syntax
`<number> | inherit`

Initial Value
50

Percentages
n/a

Inherited
yes

Applies to
all elements

Media Groups
aural

Values

<number>
Defines the range of stress inflection. The actual meaning of this value will depend on the language being spoken, as different human languages permit different ranges of stress inflection. The exact mechanism is not given in the specification. In general, higher values will lead to greater inflection on stress markers, while lower values will lessen the stress inflection.

Notes

According to the specification, `stress` refers to "the height of 'local peaks' in the intonation contour of a voice." As an example, the English language uses stress markers to highlight various parts of a sentence using primary, secondary, and tertiary stress. `stress` combines with `pitch-range` to produce the nuances of a given language.

Examples

```
strong {stress: 80;}
div.aside {stress: 40;}
```

Related Properties

`pitch-range`, `voice-family`

voice-family

`voice-family` is used to define the specific voice, and optionally a generic voice type, which is to be used in the speaking of content.

Summary

Value Syntax
```
[[<specific-voice> | <generic-voice> ],]*
[<specific-voice> | <generic-voice> ] | inherit
```

Initial Value
UA dependent

Percentages
n/a

Inherited
yes

Applies to
all elements

Media Groups
aural

Values

<specific-voice>
Any specific voice name may be declared for the voice, although those voice names with whitespace or other special characters in their names should be quoted.

<generic-voice>
The permitted generic voice family values are `male`, `female`, and `child`.

Notes
In effect, `voice-family` is the equivalent of `font-family` for aural media.

Examples
```
body {voice-family: JoeBob, Cuthbert, male;}
*.fem {voice-family: Julie, "Ma Bell", Aenea, female;}
```

Related Properties
`pitch`, `pitch-range`, `stress`, `richness`

volume

`volume` describes the "loudness" of a sound.

Summary

Value Syntax
`<number>` | `<percentage>` | `silent` | `x-soft` | `soft` | `medium` | `loud` | `x-loud` | `inherit`

Initial Value
`medium`

Percentages
refer to inherited value

Inherited
yes

Applies to
all elements

Media Groups
aural

Values

<number>

Any number in the range $0 - 100$. The actual decibel levels which correspond to the `volume` number values 0 and 100 are meant to be set by the user agent. For this reason, the specification defines the number 0 as the *minimum audible* level, and 100 as the *maximum comfortable* level. This is due to the fact that different environments require different decibel ranges for comfortable hearing. For example, the setting for 0 should be different when driving in a car than the setting in a home office; similarly, the setting for 100 will be different in a library than in a teenager's bedroom. This approach allows users to set the volume range appropriate for their diverse environments while still making use of the same author stylesheet. This also means that the value 0 will produce some sound, at whatever decibel level is set to be the minimum audible level for the current user environment.

<percentage>

Percentage values are calculated relative to the inherited value of `volume`, and then clipped to the range $0 - 100$ if necessary.

silent

No sound should be produced. Thus, `silent` and 0 are *not* equivalent, as 0 could produce a 30-decibel sound or a 5-decibel sound, depending on the user agent's settings. Like the mute button on a television, `silent` will always result in a lack of any sound, regardless of the user agent settings. However, the time it would normally have taken to play the sound (or read the text) will be filled with silence. In other words, the user agent still attempts to play a sound or read text, but produces no actual sound. This is somewhat equivalent to the visual style `visibility: hidden`, which causes elements to be invisible but take up the space which would be required to display them.

x-soft

Equivalent to the numeric value 0.

soft

Equivalent to the numeric value 25.

medium

Equivalent to the numeric value 50.

loud

Equivalent to the numeric value 75.

x-loud
Equivalent to the numeric value `100`.

Notes

In more precise terms, `volume`, to quote the specification, sets "the median volume of the waveform... In other words, a highly inflected voice at a volume of 50 might peak well above that." Thus, `volume` does not enforce exactly the same volume level for every sound produced, but instead defines the midpoint of the sounds which are produced. In addition, the property `volume` is intended to adjust the dynamic range of a sound, since it cannot be expected to override physical controls like volume knobs.

Examples

```
div.sotto {volume: 33;}
h1 {volume: loud;}
*.quiet {volume: 0;}
*.mute {volume: silent;}
```

Related Properties

`speak`

Part II
Summaries

Chapter 7
Browser Compatibility

It is the unfortunate truth that CSS support in Web browsers has not been perfect. Only recently have browsers even begun to reach a full and correct implementation of CSS1, and thus turned their eyes to implementing CSS2. Knowing the potential trouble spots can save authors a great deal of frustration. As of this writing, CSS2 support was not advanced enough to merit its own chart. In fact, the only portions of CSS2 which could reasonably be charted are selectors (minimal adoption) and positioning (bugs galore). The rest of CSS2 is either not supported, or partially supported. It is true that Navigator 6 and Opera 5 have pretty good CSS2 support, but they also have pretty poor market penetration. Thus, we have undertaken to chart support for the part of CSS which has the widest acceptance: CSS1.

In the following chart, each property and value is given a support rating for each browser on the chart. These ratings are explained in Table 7-1.

The number found next to each property name below refers to the section number in the CSS1 specification.

Rating	Description
Y	Yes, the property is supported in this browser. No known bugs exist, and the browser's behavior is in accordance with the CSS specification.
Q	Quirks still exist in this browser's support, but overall it is very good. This rating is reserved for browsers which are very, very close to matching the specification, or which follow the specification's letter but not its spirit.
P	Partial implementation of the specification. This generally means that while there are no bugs in the browser's behavior, there are also gaps in its support.
B	Buggy implementation. Not only is the support incomplete, it is incorrect and may do great violence to page layout.
N	No support for this property or value. The browser will act as if the property or value did not exist.

Table 7-1.   Support Chart Ratings Explained

Basic Concepts

Property or Value	Windows95								Macintosh				
	Nav4	Nav6	IE4	IE5	IE55	Op3	Op4	Op5	Nav4	Nav6	IE4	IE5	
1.1 Containment in HTML	P	Y	Q	Q	Q	Y	Y	Y	P	Y	Y	Y	*
LINK	Y	Y	Y	Y	Y	Y	Y	Y	Y	Y	Y	Y	
<STYLE>...</STYLE>	Y	Y	Y	Y	Y	Y	Y	Y	Y	Y	Y	Y	*
@import	N	Y	Q	Q	Q	Y	Y	Y	N	Y	Y	Y	
<x STYLE="dec;">	B	Y	Y	Y	Y	Y	Y	Y	B	Y	Y	Y	
1.2 Grouping	Y	Y	Y	Y	Y	Y	Y	Y	Y	Y	Y	Y	
x, y, z {dec;}	Y	Y	Y	Y	Y	Y	Y	Y	Y	Y	Y	Y	
1.3 Inheritance	B	Y	Y	Y	Y	Y	Y	Y	B	Y	Y	Y	*
(inherited values)	B	Y	Y	Y	Y	Y	Y	Y	B	Y	Y	Y	
1.4 Class selector	Y	Y	Q	Q	Q	Y	Y	Y	Y	Y	Y	Y	*
class	Y	Y	Q	Q	Q	Y	Y	Y	Y	Y	Y	Y	
1.5 ID selector	B	Y	B	B	B	Y	Y	Y	B	Y	B	B	*
#ID	B	Y	B	B	B	B	Y	Y	B	Y	B	Y	
1.6 Contextual selectors	Y	Y	Y	Y	Y	Y	Y	Y	B	Y	Y	Y	*
x y z {dec;}	Y	Y	Y	Y	Y	Y	Y	Y	B	Y	Y	Y	
1.7 Comments	Y	Y	Y	Y	Y	Y	Y	Y	Y	Y	Y	Y	
/* comment */	Y	Y	Y	Y	Y	Y	Y	Y	Y	Y	Y	Y	

Pseudo-classes and Pseudo-elements

Property or Value		Windows95								Macintosh			
		Nav4	Nav6	IE4	IE5	IE55	Op3	Op4	Op5	Nav4	Nav6	IE4	IE5
2.1	anchor	P	Y	Y	Y	Y	P	P	Y	P	Y	Y	Y
	:link	Y	Y	Y	Y	Y	Y	Y	Y	Y	Y	Y	Y
	:active	N	Y	Y	Y	Y	N	N	Y	N	Y	Y	Y
	:visited	N	Y	Y	Y	Y	Y	N	Y	N	Y	Y	Y
2.3	first-line	N	Y	N	N	Y	Y	Y	Y	N	Y	N	Y *
	:first-line	N	Y	N	N	Y	Y	Y	Y	N	Y	N	Y
2.4	first-letter	N	Y	N	N	Y	Y	Y	Y	N	Y	N	Y *
	:first-letter	N	Y	N	N	Y	Y	Y	Y	N	Y	N	Y

The Cascade

Property or Value		Windows95								Macintosh			
		Nav4	Nav6	IE4	IE5	IE55	Op3	Op4	Op5	Nav4	Nav6	IE4	IE5
3.1	important	N	Y	Y	Y	Y	Y	Y	Y	N	Y	N	Y
	!important	N	Y	Y	Y	Y	Y	Y	Y	N	Y	N	Y
3.2	Cascading order	B	Y	Y	Y	Y	Y	Y	Y	B	Y	Y	Y *
	Weight sorting	B	Y	Y	Y	Y	Y	Y	Y	B	Y	Y	Y
	Origin sorting	B	Y	Y	Y	Y	Y	Y	Y	B	Y	Y	Y
	Specificity sorting	B	Y	Y	Y	Y	Y	Y	Y	B	Y	Y	Y
	Order sorting	B	Y	Y	Y	Y	Y	Y	Y	B	Y	Y	Y

Font Properties

Property or Value	Windows95								Macintosh			
	Nav4	Nav6	IE4	IE5	IE55	Op3	Op4	Op5	Nav4	Nav6	IE4	IE5
5.2.2 font-family	Y	Y	Y	Y	Y	Y	Y	Y	Y	Y	Y	Y
<family-name>	Y	Y	Y	Y	Y	Y	Y	Y	Y	Y	Y	Y
<generic-family>	P	Y	Y	Y	Y	Y	Y	Y	Y	Y	Y	Y
serif	Y	Y	Y	Y	Y	Y	Y	Y	Y	Y	Y	Y
sans-serif	Y	Y	Y	Y	Y	Y	Y	Y	Y	Y	Y	Y
cursive	N	Y	Y	Y	Y	Y	Y	Y	Y	Y	Y	Y *
fantasy	N	Y	Y	Y	Y	Y	Y	Y	Y	Y	Y	Y
monospace	Y	Y	Y	Y	Y	Y	Y	Y	Y	Y	Y	Y
5.2.3 font-style	P	Y	Y	Y	Y	Y	Y	Y	P	Y	Y	Y
normal	Y	Y	Y	Y	Y	Y	Y	Y	Y	Y	Y	Y
italic	Y	Y	Y	Y	Y	Y	Y	Y	Y	Y	Y	Y
oblique	N	Y	Y	Y	Y	Y	Y	Y	N	Y	Y	Y
5.2.4 font-variant	N	Y	Q	Q	Q	Y	Y	Y	N	Y	Q	Y
normal	N	Y	Y	Y	Y	Y	Y	Y	N	Y	Y	Y
small-caps	N	Y	Q	Q	Q	Y	Y	Y	N	Y	Q	Y
5.2.5 font-weight	P	Y	Y	Y	Y	Y	Y	Y	P	Y	Y	Y *
normal	Y	Y	Y	Y	Y	Y	Y	Y	Y	Y	Y	Y
bold	Y	Y	Y	Y	Y	Y	Y	Y	Y	Y	Y	Y
bolder	Y	Y	Y	Y	Y	Y	Y	Y	N	Y	Y	Y
lighter	N	Y	Y	Y	Y	Y	Y	Y	N	Y	Y	Y
100 - 900	Y	Y	Y	Y	Y	Y	Y	Y	Y	Y	Y	Y

Font Properties

Property or Value	Windows95								Macintosh			
	Nav4	Nav6	IE4	IE5	IE55	Op3	Op4	Op5	Nav4	Nav6	IE4	IE5
5.2.6 font-size	Y	Y	P	P	P	Y	Y	Y	Y	Y	Q	Y
<absolute-size>	Y	Y	Q	Q	Q	Y	Y	Y	Y	Y	Q	Y
xx-small - xx-large	Y	Y	Q	Q	Q	Y	Y	Q	Y	Y	Q	Y *
<relative-size>	Y	Y	Y	Y	B	Y	Y	Y	Y	Y	Y	Y
larger	Y	Y	Y	Y	B	Y	Y	Y	Y	Y	Y	Y
smaller	Y	Y	Y	Y	B	Y	Y	Y	Y	Y	Y	Y
<length>	Y	Y	Y	Y	Y	Y	Y	Y	Y	Y	Y	Y
<percentage>	Y	Y	Y	Y	Y	Y	Y	Y	Y	Y	Y	Y
5.2.7 font	P	Y	P	P	Y	Y	Y	Y	P	Y	Q	Y
<font-family>	P	Y	Y	Y	Y	Y	Y	Y	Y	Y	Y	Y
<font-style>	P	Y	Y	Y	Y	Y	Y	Y	Y	Y	Y	Y
<font-variant>	N	Y	Q	Q	Q	Y	Y	Y	N	Y	Q	Y
<font-weight>	P	Y	Y	Y	P	Y	Y	Y	Y	Y	Y	Y
<font-size>	Y	Y	Q	Q	Q	Y	Y	Y	Y	Y	Y	Y
<line-height>	B	Y	Y	Y	Y	Y	Y	Y	B	Y	Y	Y

Color and Background Properties

Property or Value		Windows95								Macintosh				
		Nav4	Nav6	IE4	IE5	IE55	Op3	Op4	Op5	Nav4	Nav6	IE4	IE5	
5.3.1	color	Y	Y	Y	Y	Y	Y	Y	Y	Y	Y	Y	Y	
	<color>	Y	Y	Y	Y	Y	Y	Y	Y	Y	Y	Y	Y	
5.3.2	background-color	B	Y	Y	Y	Y	Y	Y	Y	B	Y	Y	Y	
	<color>	B	Y	Y	Y	Y	Y	Y	Y	B	Y	Y	Y	*
	transparent	B	Y	Y	Y	Y	Y	B	Y	B	Y	Y	Y	*
5.3.3	background-image	Y	Y	Y	Y	Y	Y	B	Y	Y	Y	Y	Y	
	<url>	Y	Y	Y	Y	Y	Y	Y	Y	Y	Y	Y	Y	
	none	Y	Y	Y	Y	Y	Y	Y	Y	Y	Y	Y	Y	
5.3.4	background-repeat	P	Y	P	Y	Y	Y	Y	Y	B	Y	Y	Y	
	repeat	Y	Y	B	Y	Y	Y	Y	Y	Y	Y	Y	Y	*
	repeat-x	P	Y	B	Y	Y	Y	Y	Y	P	Y	Y	Y	*
	repeat-y	P	Y	B	Y	Y	Y	Y	Y	P	Y	Y	Y	*
	no-repeat	Y	Y	Y	Y	Y	Y	Y	Y	Y	Y	Y	Y	
5.3.5	background-attachment	N	Y	Y	Y	Y	N	Y	Y	N	Y	Y	Y	
	scroll	N	Y	Y	Y	Y	N	Y	Y	N	Y	Y	Y	
	fixed	N	Y	Y	Y	Y	N	Y	Y	N	Y	Y	Y	

Color and Background Properties

Property or Value		Windows95								Macintosh			
		Nav4	Nav6	IE4	IE5	IE55	Op3	Op4	Op5	Nav4	Nav6	IE4	IE5
5.3.6	background-position	N	Y	Y	Y	Y	Y	Y	Y	N	Y	Y	Y
	\<percentage\>	N	Y	Y	Y	Y	Y	Y	Y	N	Y	Y	Y
	\<length\>	N	Y	Y	Y	Y	Y	Y	Y	N	Y	Y	Y
	top	N	Y	Y	Y	Y	Y	Y	Y	N	Y	Y	Y
	center	N	Y	Y	Y	Y	Y	Y	Y	N	Y	Y	Y
	bottom	N	Y	Y	Y	Y	Y	Y	Y	N	Y	Y	Y
	left	N	Y	Y	Y	Y	Y	Y	Y	N	Y	Y	Y
	right	N	Y	Y	Y	Y	Y	Y	Y	N	Y	Y	Y *
5.3.7	background	P	Y	P	Y	Y	P	P	Y	P	Y	Y	Y
	\<background-color\>	B	Y	Y	Y	Y	Y	Y	Y	P	Y	Y	Y
	\<background-image\>	P	Y	Y	Y	Y	Y	Y	Y	P	Y	Y	Y
	\<background-repeat\>	P	Y	B	Y	Y	Y	Y	Y	P	Y	Y	Y
	\<background-attachment\>	N	Y	Y	Y	Y	N	Y	Y	N	Y	Y	Y
	\<background-position\>	N	Y	Y	Y	Y	Y	Y	Y	N	Y	Y	Y

7

Text Properties

Property or Value		Windows95								Macintosh			
		Nav4	Nav6	IE4	IE5	IE55	Op3	Op4	Op5	Nav4	Nav6	IE4	IE5
5.4.1	word-spacing	N	Y	N	N	N	Y	Y	Y	N	Y	Y	Y
	normal	N	Y	N	N	N	Y	Y	Y	N	Y	Y	Y
	<length>	N	Y	N	N	N	Y	Y	Y	N	Y	Y	Y
5.4.2	letter-spacing	N	Y	Y	Y	Y	Y	Y	Y	N	Y	Y	Y
	normal	N	Y	Y	Y	Y	Y	Y	Y	N	Y	Y	Y
	<length>	N	Y	Y	Y	Y	Y	Y	Y	N	Y	Y	Y
5.4.3	text-decoration	B	B	B	B	B	B	B	B	B	B	B	P
	none	Q	Y	Y	Y	Y	Y	Y	Y	Q	Y	Q	Y
	underline	Q	Y	Y	Y	Y	Y	Y	Y	Q	Y	Q	Y *
	overline	N	Y	Y	Y	Y	Y	Y	Y	N	Y	Y	Y
	line-through	Y	Y	Y	Y	Y	Y	Y	Y	Y	Y	Y	Y
	blink	Y	Y	N	N	N	N	Y	Y	Y	Y	N	N *
5.4.4	vertical-align	N	Y	P	P	P	P	Y	Y	N	Y	P	Y
	baseline	N	Y	Y	Y	Y	Y	Y	Y	N	Y	Y	Y
	sub	N	Y	Y	Y	Y	Y	Y	Y	N	Y	Y	Y
	super	N	Y	Y	Y	Y	Y	Y	Y	N	Y	Y	Y
	top	N	Y	N	N	N	B	Y	Y	N	Y	Y	Y
	text-top	N	Y	N	N	N	N	Y	Y	N	Y	Y	Y
	middle	N	Y	B	B	B	B	Y	Y	N	Y	Y	Y
	bottom	N	Y	N	N	N	B	Y	Y	N	Y	B	Y
	text-bottom	N	Y	N	N	N	B	Y	Y	N	Y	B	Y
	<percentage>	N	Y	N	N	N	Y	Y	Y	N	Y	B	Y

Text Properties

Property or Value		Windows95								Macintosh			
		Nav4	Nav6	IE4	IE5	IE55	Op3	Op4	Op5	Nav4	Nav6	IE4	IE5
5.4.5	text-transform	Y	Y	Y	Y	Y	P	Y	Y	Y	Y	Y	Y
	capitalize	Y	Y	Y	Y	Y	Y	Y	Y	Y	Y	Y	Y
	uppercase *	Y	Y	Y	Y	Y	B	Y	Y	Y	Y	Y	Y
	lowercase	Y	Y	Y	Y	Y	Y	Y	Y	Y	Y	Y	Y
	none	Y	Y	Y	Y	Y	Y	Y	Y	Y	Y	Y	Y
5.4.6	text-align	Y	Y	Y	Y	Y	Y	Y	Y	P	Y	P	Y
	left	Y	Y	Y	Y	Y	Y	Y	Y	Y	Y	Y	Y
	right *	Y	Y	Y	Y	Y	Y	Y	Y	Y	Y	Y	Y
	center	Y	Y	Y	Y	Y	Y	Y	Y	Y	Y	Y	Y
	justify *	B	Y	Y	Y	Y	Y	Y	Y	B	Y	N	Y
5.4.7	text-indent *	Y	Y	Y	Y	Y	Y	Y	Y	Y	Y	Y	Y
	<length>	Y	Y	Y	Y	Y	Y	Y	Y	Y	Y	Y	Y
	<percentage>	Y	Y	Y	Y	Y	Y	Y	Y	Y	Y	Y	Y
5.4.8	line-height *	P	Y	Y	Y	Y	Q	Y	Y	P	Y	P	Y
	normal	Y	Y	Y	Y	Y	Y	Y	Y	Y	Y	Y	Y
	<number>	P	Y	Y	Y	Y	Y	Y	Y	P	Y	Y	Y
	<length>	B	Y	Y	Y	Y	Y	Y	Y	B	Y	B	Y
	<percentage>	P	Y	Y	Y	Y	Y	Y	Y	P	Y	Y	Y

7

Box Properties

Property or Value		Windows95								Macintosh				
		Nav4	Nav6	IE4	IE5	IE55	Op3	Op4	Op5	Nav4	Nav6	IE4	IE5	
5.5.01	margin-top	P	Y	P	P	Y	Y	Y	Y	P	Y	P	Y	*
	<length>	P	Y	P	P	Y	Y	Y	Y	P	Y	P	Y	
	<percentage>	P	Y	P	P	Y	Y	Y	Y	P	Y	P	Y	
	auto	P	Y	P	P	Y	Y	Y	Y	P	Y	P	Y	
5.5.02	margin-right	B	B	B	P	Q	B	B	Y	B	B	P	Y	*
	<length>	B	Y	B	P	Y	Y	Y	Y	B	Y	P	Y	
	<percentage>	B	Y	B	P	Y	Y	Y	Y	B	Y	P	Y	
	auto	N	Y	N	N	Y	Y	Y	Y	N	Y	P	Y	
5.5.03	margin-bottom	N	Y	N	P	Y	Y	Y	Y	N	Y	P	Y	*
	<length>	N	Y	N	P	Y	Y	Y	Y	N	Y	P	Y	
	<percentage>	N	Y	N	P	Y	Y	Y	Y	N	Y	P	Y	
	auto	N	Y	N	P	Y	Y	Y	Y	N	Y	P	Y	
5.5.04	margin-left	B	Y	B	P	Y	B	B	Y	B	Y	P	Y	*
	<length>	B	Y	B	P	Y	Y	Y	Y	B	Y	P	Y	
	<percentage>	B	Y	B	P	Y	Y	Y	Y	B	Y	P	Y	
	auto	N	Y	N	N	Y	Y	Y	Y	N	Y	P	Y	
5.5.05	margin	B	B	B	P	Y	B	B	Y	B	B	P	Y	*
	<length>	B	Y	B	P	Y	Y	Y	Y	B	Y	P	Y	
	<percentage>	B	Y	B	P	Y	Y	Y	Y	B	Y	P	Y	
	auto	N	Y	N	P	Y	Y	Y	Y	N	Y	P	Y	

Box Properties

Property or Value		Windows95								Macintosh				
		Nav4	Nav6	IE4	IE5	IE55	Op3	Op4	Op5	Nav4	Nav6	IE4	IE5	
5.5.06	padding-top	B	Y	P	P	Q	Y	Y	Y	B	Y	P	Y	*
	<length>	B	Y	P	P	Y	Y	Y	Y	B	Y	P	Y	
	<percentage>	B	Y	P	P	Y	Y	Y	Y	B	Y	P	Y	
5.5.07	padding-right	B	Y	P	P	Q	Y	Y	Y	B	Y	P	Y	*
	<length>	B	Y	P	P	Y	Y	Y	Y	B	Y	P	Y	
	<percentage>	B	Y	P	P	Y	Y	Y	Y	B	Y	P	Y	
5.5.08	padding-bottom	B	Y	P	P	Y	Y	Y	Y	B	Y	P	Y	*
	<length>	B	Y	P	P	Y	Y	Y	Y	B	Y	P	Y	
	<percentage>	B	Y	P	P	Y	Y	Y	Y	B	Y	P	Y	
5.5.09	padding-left	B	Y	P	P	Y	Y	Y	Y	B	Y	P	Y	*
	<length>	B	Y	P	P	Y	Y	Y	Y	B	Y	P	Y	
	<percentage>	B	Y	P	P	Y	Y	Y	Y	B	Y	P	Y	
5.5.10	padding	B	Y	P	P	Q	B	B	Y	B	Y	P	Y	*
	<length>	B	Y	P	P	Y	B	B	Y	B	Y	P	Y	
	<percentage>	B	Y	P	P	Y	B	B	Y	B	Y	P	Y	
5.5.11	border-top-width	B	Y	P	P	Y	Y	Y	Y	B	Y	P	Y	*
	thin	Y	Y	P	P	Y	Y	Y	Y	Y	Y	P	Y	
	medium	Y	Y	P	P	Y	Y	Y	Y	Y	Y	P	Y	
	thick	Y	Y	P	P	Y	Y	Y	Y	Y	Y	P	Y	
	<length>	Y	Y	P	P	Y	Y	Y	Y	Y	Y	P	Y	

7

Box Properties

Property or Value		Windows95					Op3	Op4	Op5	Macintosh				
		Nav4	Nav6	IE4	IE5	IE55				Nav4	Nav6	IE4	IE5	
5.5.12	border-right-width	B	Y	P	P	Y	Y	Y	Y	B	Y	P	Y	*
	thin	Y	Y	P	P	Y	Y	Y	Y	Y	Y	P	Y	
	medium	Y	Y	P	P	Y	Y	Y	Y	Y	Y	P	Y	
	thick	Y	Y	P	P	Y	Y	Y	Y	Y	Y	P	Y	
	<length>	Y	Y	P	P	Y	Y	Y	Y	Y	Y	P	Y	
5.5.13	border-bottom-width	B	Y	P	P	Y	Y	Y	Y	B	Y	P	Y	*
	thin	B	Y	P	P	Y	Y	Y	Y	B	Y	P	Y	
	medium	B	Y	P	P	Y	Y	Y	Y	B	Y	P	Y	
	thick	B	Y	P	P	Y	Y	Y	Y	B	Y	P	Y	
	<length>	B	Y	P	P	Y	Y	Y	Y	B	Y	P	Y	
5.5.14	border-left-width	B	Y	P	P	Y	Y	Y	Y	B	Y	P	Y	*
	thin	Y	Y	P	P	Y	Y	Y	Y	Y	Y	P	Y	
	medium	Y	Y	P	P	Y	Y	Y	Y	Y	Y	P	Y	
	thick	Y	Y	P	P	Y	Y	Y	Y	Y	Y	P	Y	
	<length>	Y	Y	P	P	Y	Y	Y	Y	Y	Y	P	Y	
5.5.15	border-width	B	Y	P	P	Y	Y	Y	Y	B	Y	P	Y	*
	thin	Y	Y	P	P	Y	Y	Y	Y	Y	Y	P	Y	
	medium	Y	Y	P	P	Y	Y	Y	Y	Y	Y	P	Y	
	thick	Y	Y	P	P	Y	Y	Y	Y	Y	Y	P	Y	
	<length>	Y	Y	P	P	Y	Y	Y	Y	Y	Y	P	Y	

Box Properties

	Property or Value	Windows95								Macintosh			
		Nav4	Nav6	IE4	IE5	IE55	Op3	Op4	Op5	Nav4	Nav6	IE4	IE5
5.5.16	border-color	P	Y	Y	Y	Y	Y	Y	Y	P	Y	Y	Y *
	<color>	P	Y	Y	Y	Y	Y	Y	Y	P	Y	Y	Y
5.5.17	border-style	P	Y	P	P	Y	Y	Y	Y	P	Y	Y	Y *
	none	Y	Y	Y	Y	Y	Y	Y	Y	Y	Y	Y	Y
	dotted	N	Y	N	N	Y	Y	Y	Y	N	Y	Y	Y
	dashed	N	Y	N	N	Y	Y	Y	Y	N	Y	Y	Y
	solid	Y	Y	Y	Y	Y	Y	Y	Y	Y	Y	Y	Y
	double	Y	Y	Y	Y	Y	Y	Y	Y	Y	Y	Y	Y
	groove	Y	Y	Y	Y	Y	Y	Y	Y	Y	Y	Y	Y
	ridge	Y	Y	Y	Y	Y	Y	Y	Y	Y	Y	Y	Y
	inset	Y	Y	Y	Y	Y	Y	Y	Y	Y	Y	Y	Y
	outset	Y	Y	Y	Y	Y	Y	Y	Y	Y	Y	Y	Y
5.5.18	border-top	N	Y	P	P	Y	P	Y	Y	N	Y	P	Y *
	<border-top-width>	N	Y	P	P	Y	P	Y	Y	N	Y	P	Y
	<border-style>	N	Y	P	P	Y	P	Y	Y	N	Y	P	Y
	<color>	N	Y	P	P	Y	P	Y	Y	N	Y	P	Y
5.5.19	border-right	N	Y	P	P	Y	P	Y	Y	N	Y	P	Y *
	<border-right-width>	N	Y	P	P	Y	P	Y	Y	N	Y	P	Y
	<border-style>	N	Y	P	P	Y	P	Y	Y	N	Y	P	Y
	<color>	N	Y	P	P	Y	P	Y	Y	N	Y	P	Y

7

Box Properties

Property or Value		Windows95								Macintosh				
		Nav4	Nav6	IE4	IE5	IE55	Op3	Op4	Op5	Nav4	Nav6	IE4	IE5	
5.5.20	border-bottom	N	Y	P	P	Y	P	Y	Y	N	Y	P	Y	*
	<border-bottom-width>	N	Y	P	P	Y	P	Y	Y	N	Y	P	Y	
	<border-style>	N	Y	P	P	Y	P	Y	Y	N	Y	P	Y	
	<color>	N	Y	P	P	Y	P	Y	Y	N	Y	P	Y	
5.5.21	border-left	N	Y	P	P	Y	P	Y	Y	N	Y	P	Y	*
	<border-left-width>	N	Y	P	P	Y	P	Y	Y	N	Y	P	Y	
	<border-style>	N	Y	P	P	Y	P	Y	Y	N	Y	P	Y	
	<color>	N	Y	P	P	Y	P	Y	Y	N	Y	P	Y	
5.5.22	Border	P	Y	P	P	Y	P	Y	B	P	Y	P	Y	*
	<border-width>	B	Y	P	P	Y	P	Y	Y	B	Y	P	Y	
	<border-style>	P	Y	P	P	Y	P	Y	Y	P	Y	P	Y	
	<color>	Y	Y	P	P	Y	P	Y	Y	Y	Y	P	Y	
5.5.23	Width	P	Y	P	P	Y	Q	Y	Y	P	Y	P	Y	*
	<length>	P	Y	P	P	Y	Q	Y	Y	P	Y	P	Y	
	<percentage>	P	Y	P	P	Y	Q	Y	Y	P	Y	P	Y	
	Auto	P	Y	P	P	Y	Q	Y	Y	P	Y	P	Y	

Box Properties

Property or Value		Windows95								Macintosh			
		Nav4	Nav6	IE4	IE5	IE55	Op3	Op4	Op5	Nav4	Nav6	IE4	IE5
5.5.24	Height	N	Y	Y	Y	Y	Y	Y	Y	N	Y	Y	Y
	<length>	N	Y	Y	Y	Y	Y	Y	Y	N	Y	Y	Y
	Auto	N	Y	Y	Y	Y	Y	Y	Y	N	Y	Y	Y
5.5.25	Float	P	Y	P	P	Q	B	Q	Y	P	Y	B	Q *
	Left	B	Y	B	B	Y	Y	Y	Y	B	Y	Y	Y
	Right	B	Y	B	B	Y	Y	Y	Y	B	Y	Y	Y
	None	Y	Y	Y	Y	Y	Y	Y	Y	Y	Y	Y	Y
5.5.26	Clear	P	Y	P	P	Y	B	Y	Y	P	Y	Y	Y *
	None	Y	Y	Y	Y	Y	Y	Y	Y	Y	Y	Y	Y
	Left	B	Y	B	B	Y	N	Y	Y	B	Y	Y	Y
	Right	B	Y	B	B	Y	Y	Y	Y	B	Y	Y	Y
	Both	Y	Y	Y	Y	Y	Y	Y	Y	Y	Y	Y	Y

Classification Properties

Property or Value	Windows95								Macintosh			
	Nav4	Nav6	IE4	IE5	IE55	Op3	Op4	Op5	Nav4	Nav6	IE4	IE5
5.6.1 Display	P	Y	P	P	P	P	Y	Y	P	Y	P	Y
Block	B	Y	N	Y	Y	Y	Y	Y	B	Y	P	Y
Inline	N	Y	N	Y	Y	B	Y	Y	N	Y	N	Y
list-item	B	Y	N	N	N	N	Y	Y	P	Y	P	Y *
None	Y	Y	Y	Y	Y	Y	Y	Y	Y	Y	Y	Y
5.6.2 white-space	P	Y	N	N	P	N	Y	Y	P	Y	N	Y
Normal	Y	Y	N	N	Y	N	Y	Y	Y	Y	N	Y
Pre	Y	Y	N	N	Y	N	Y	Y	Y	Y	N	Y
Nowrap	N	Y	N	N	Y	N	Y	Y	N	Y	N	Y
5.6.3 list-style-type	Y	Y	Y	Y	Y	Y	Y	Y	P	Y	Y	Y
Disc	Y	Y	Y	Y	Y	Y	Y	Y	Y	Y	Y	Y
Circle	Y	Y	Y	Y	Y	Y	Y	Y	Y	Y	Y	Y
Square	Y	Y	Y	Y	Y	Y	Y	Y	Y	Y	Y	Y
Decimal	Y	Y	Y	Y	Y	Y	Y	Y	Y	Y	Y	Y
lower-roman	Y	Y	Y	Y	Y	Y	Y	Y	Y	Y	Y	Y
upper-roman	Y	Y	Y	Y	Y	Y	Y	Y	Y	Y	Y	Y
lower-alpha	Y	Y	Y	Y	Y	Y	Y	Y	Y	Y	Y	Y
upper-alpha	Y	Y	Y	Y	Y	Y	Y	Y	B	Y	Y	Y
None	Y	Y	Y	Y	Y	Y	Y	Y	Y	Y	Y	Y *

7

Classification Properties

Property or Value	Windows95								Macintosh			
	Nav4	Nav6	IE4	IE5	IE55	Op3	Op4	Op5	Nav4	Nav6	IE4	IE5
5.6.4 list-style-image	N	Y	Y	Y	Y	Y	Y	Y	N	Y	Y	Y
<url>	N	Y	Y	Y	Y	Y	Y	Y	N	Y	Y	Y
None	N	Y	Y	Y	Y	Y	Y	Y	N	Y	Y	Y
5.6.5 list-style-position	N	Y	Y	Y	Y	Y	Y	Y	N	Y	Y	Y *
Inside	N	Y	Y	Y	Y	Y	Y	Y	N	Y	Q	Y
Outside	N	Y	Y	Y	Y	Y	Y	Y	N	Y	Y	Y
5.6.6 list-style	P	Y	P	Y	Y	Y	Y	Y	P	Y	P	Y
<keyword>	Y	Y	Y	Y	Y	Y	Y	Y	P	Y	Y	Y
<position>	N	Y	Q	Q	Y	Y	Y	Y	N	Y	Q	Y
<url>	N	Y	Y	Y	Y	Y	Y	Y	N	Y	Y	Y

Units

Property or Value		Windows95								Macintosh			
		Nav4	Nav6	IE4	IE5	IE55	Op3	Op4	Op5	Nav4	Nav6	IE4	IE5
6.1	Length Units	P	Y	Y	Y	Y	Y	Y	Y	Y	Y	Y	Y *
	Em	Y	Y	Y	Y	Y	Y	Y	Y	Y	Y	Y	Y
	Ex	Q	Y	Q	Q	Y	Q	Y	Y	Q	Y	Q	Y
	Px	Y	Y	Y	Y	Y	Y	Y	Y	Y	Y	Y	Y
	In	Y	Y	Y	Y	Y	Y	Y	Y	Y	Y	Y	Y
	Cm	Y	Y	Y	Y	Y	Y	Y	Y	Y	Y	Y	Y
	Mm	Y	Y	Y	Y	Y	Y	Y	Y	Y	Y	Y	Y
	Pt	Y	Y	Y	Y	Y	Y	Y	Y	Y	Y	Y	Y
	Pc	Y	Y	Y	Y	Y	Y	Y	Y	Y	Y	Y	Y
6.2	Percentage Units	Y	Y	Y	Y	Y	Y	Y	Y	Y	Y	Y	Y
	<percentage>	Y	Y	Y	Y	Y	Y	Y	Y	Y	Y	Y	Y
6.3	Color Units	P	Y	Y	Y	Y	Y	Y	Y	P	Y	Y	Y
	#000	Y	Y	Y	Y	Y	Y	Y	Y	Y	Y	Y	Y
	#000000	Y	Y	Y	Y	Y	Y	Y	Y	Y	Y	Y	Y
	(RRR,GGG,BBB)	Y	Y	Y	Y	Y	Y	Y	Y	Y	Y	Y	Y
	(R%,G%,B%)	Y	Y	Y	Y	Y	Y	Y	Y	Y	Y	Y	Y
	<keyword>	B	Y	Y	Y	Y	Y	Y	Y	B	Y	Y	Y
6.4	URLs	B	Y	Y	Y	Y	Y	Y	Y	B	Y	Y	Y *
	<url>	B	Y	Y	Y	Y	Y	Y	Y	B	Y	Y	Y *

Notes

1.1 Containment in HTML

@import

WinIE4 and WinIE5 both import files even when the `@import` statement is at the end of the document stylesheet. This is technically in violation of the CSS1 specification, although obviously not a major failing; thus the "Quirk" rating.

1.1 Containment in HTML

<x STYLE="dec;">

Navigator 4 has particular trouble with list items, which is most of the reason for the "B" rating.

1.3 Inheritance

Navigator 4's inheritance is unstable at best, and fatally flawed at worst. It would take too long to list all occurrences, but particularly troublesome areas include tables and lists.

1.4 Class Selector

WinIE4/5 allows class names to begin with digits; this is not permitted under CSS1.

1.5 ID Selector

WinIE4/5 allows ID names to begin with digits; this is not permitted under CSS1. All browsers apply the style for a given ID to more than one instance of that ID in an HTML document, which is not permitted. This is an error-checking problem, not a failing of the CSS implementations, but it is significant enough to warrant the ratings shown. Note that ID and classes can begin with digits under CSS2, so this is not as much of a problem as it might first appear.

7

1.6 Contextual Selectors

x y z {dec;}
MacNav4 has the most trouble with contextual selectors involving tables. For example, HTML BODY TABLE P is not properly handled.

3.2 Cascading Order

There are simply far too many instances of problems, with far too many of them defying analysis, to list here.

5.2.2 font-family

cursive
Despite having a preferences setting for cursive fonts, Opera does not seem to apply the preference, but instead substitutes another font.

5.2.4 font-variant

small-caps
WinIE4/5 approximates the small-caps style by making all such text uppercase. While this can be justified under the CSS1 specification, visually it does not render the text in small caps.

5.2.6 font-size

xx-small - xx-large
IE4/5's (both Win and Mac) values for absolute sizes assign small to be the same size as unstyled text, instead of medium, as one might expect. Thus, declaring an absolute font size (such as font-size: medium) will almost certainly lead to different size fonts in Navigator and Explorer. While this is not incorrect under the specification, it is confusing to many authors.

5.3.2 background-color

<color>
Nav4 does not apply the background color to the entire content box and padding, but rather just to the text in the element. This can be worked around by declaring a zero-width border.

5.3.2 background-color

transparent
Nav4 insists on applying this value to the parent of an element, not the element itself. This can lead to "holes" in the parent element's background. Opera 4 has a bug which only shows up when a background has been repeated, and the rest of the background of the element is transparent (either by default or when explicitly declared). Scrolling the element "offscreen" and then bringing it back can cause "holes" to be punched through the repeated images of ancestor elements, thus creating visual anomalies.

7

5.3.4 background-repeat

repeat
WinIE4 only repeats down and to the right. The correct behavior is for the background image to be tiled in both vertical directions for `repeat-y`, and both horizontal for `repeat-x`. Nav4 gets this property correct on a technicality: since it does not support `background-position`, there is no way to know whether or not it would tile in all four directions if given the chance, or instead emulate WinIE4's behavior. Opera 3.6, MacIE4/5, and WinIE5 all behave correctly.

5.3.4 background-repeat

repeat-x
WinIE4 only repeats to the right, instead of both left and right.

5.3.4 background-repeat

repeat-y
WinIE4 only repeats down, instead of both up and down.

5.3.7 background

Navigator 4.x is legendary for its inability to correctly render backgrounds. If there is no border around an element, then the background will only be visible behind the text of the element, instead of throughout the entire content-area and padding. Unfortunately, if a border is added, there will be a transparent gap between the content-area and the border itself. This is not the padding, and there is no way to get rid of the gap.

5.4.3 text-decoration

none
According to the specification, if an element is decorated, but one of its children is not, the parent's effect will still be visible on the child; in a certain sense, it "shines through." Thus, if a paragraph is underlined, but a STRONG element within it is set to have no underlining, the paragraph underline will still "span" the STRONG element. This also means that the underlining of child elements should be the same color as the parent element, unless the child element has also been set to be underlined.

In practice, however, setting an inline element to "none" will turn off all decorations, regardless of the parent's decoration. The only exceptions to this are Opera and MacIE5, which implement this part of the specification correctly. Unfortunately, Opera 4 and 5 and Netscape 6 will not "span" inline images with the text decoration of a parent element. In addition, Netscape 6 appears not to use the parent element's decoration, but instead "replicates" the underline onto child elements, which is clearly wrong. Despite its seeming simplicity, this property remains a thorny problem for browser developers.

5.4.3 text-decoration

blink

Since this value is not required under CSS1, only Navigator supports it (surprise).

5.4.5 text-transform

uppercase

Opera 3.6 uppercases the first letter in each inline element within a word, which (according to the CSS1 Test Suite) it should not do.

5.4.6 text-align

justify

In Nav4, this value has a tendency to break down in tables, but generally works in other circumstances.

5.4.8 line-height

<length>

Nav4 incorrectly permits negative values for this property.

5.4.8 line-height

Opera 3.6 applies background colors to the space between lines, as opposed to just the text itself, when the background is set for an inline element within the text. (See the CSS1 Test Suite for more details.)

5.5.01 margin-top

All margin properties seem to be problematic, or else completely unsupported, on inline elements; see `margin` in this chapter for details.

5.5.02 margin-right

All margin properties seem to be problematic, or else completely unsupported, on inline elements; see `margin` below for details. Opera 4 sometimes applies right margins to all of the boxes of an inline element, not just the last one. This seems to come and go somewhat randomly, but it is common enough to be noticeable.

5.5.03 margin-bottom

All margin properties seem to be problematic, or else completely unsupported, on inline elements; see `margin` below for details.

5.5.04 margin-left

All margin properties seem to be problematic, or else completely unsupported, on inline elements; see `margin` below for details. Opera 4 sometimes applies left margins to all of the boxes of an inline element, not just the first one. This seems to come and go somewhat randomly, but it is common enough to be noticeable.

5.5.05 margin

All margin properties seem to be problematic, or else completely unsupported, on inline elements. In the case of `margin`, support is pretty good on block-level elements in WinIE4 and WinIE5, while with inline elements, WinIE4 and WinIE5 ignore this property completely. MacIE5 correctly honors margins on all elements. Navigator 4.x does fairly well so long as margins are not applied to floating or inline elements, in which case major bugs can be tripped.

Opera 4's problems with correctly applying right and left margins to inline elements seems to get worse with `margin`.

5.5.06 padding-top

See the notes for "5.5.10 padding."

5.5.07 padding-right

See the notes for "5.5.10 padding."

5.5.08 padding-bottom

See the notes for "5.5.10 padding."

5.5.09 padding-left

See the notes for "5.5.10 padding."

5.5.10 padding

All padding properties seem to be problematic, or else completely unsupported, on inline elements. Opera 3.6 correctly ignores negative padding values, but will alter the line-height based on values of `padding` applied to inline elements, which is incorrect. WinIE4 and WinIE5 will honor padding assignments on block-level elements, but not inline elements. Navigator 4.x does fairly well so long as padding is not applied to floating or inline elements, in which case major bugs can be tripped.

5.5.11 border-top-width

See the notes for "5.5.15 border-width."

5.5.12 border-right-width

See the notes for "5.5.15 border-width."

5.5.13 border-bottom-width

See the notes for "5.5.15 border-width."

5.5.14 border-left-width

See the notes for "5.5.15 border-width."

5.5.15 border-width

Nav4 will create visible borders even when no `border-style` is set, and does not set borders on all sides when a style is set. Things get really ugly when borders are applied to inline styles. WinIE4 and WinIE5 correctly handle borders on block-level elements, but ignore them for inlines.

5.5.16 border-color

Navigator 4.x and Opera 3.6 do not set colors on individual sides, as in `border-color: red blue green purple`. Explorer cannot apply border colors to inline elements, since it does not apply borders to inlines, but this is not penalized here.

5.5.17 border-style

Navigator 4.x does not reset the `border-width` to zero if `border-style` is `none`, but instead incorrectly honors the width setting.

5.5.18 border-top

Opera 3 does not apply border styles to table elements, which is the reason for the "P" rating. IE4 and IE5 do not apply borders to inline elements.

5.5.19 border-right

Opera 3 does not apply border styles to table elements, which is the reason for the "P" rating. WinIE4 and WinIE5 do not apply borders to inline elements.

5.5.20 border-bottom

Opera 3 does not apply border styles to table elements, which is the reason for the "P" rating. IE5 and IE5/Win do not apply borders to inline elements, which is the reason for those "P" ratings.

5.5.21 border-left

Opera 3 does not apply border styles to table elements, which is the reason for the "P" rating. IE4 and IE5/Win do not apply borders to inline elements.

5.5.22 border

Opera 3 does not apply border styles to table elements, which is the reason for the "P" rating. IE4 and IE5/Win do not apply borders to inline elements, which is the reason for those "P" ratings. Opera 5 has an odd, semi-random bug that causes it to improperly place the border around the first inline element (or part thereof) in the document. The border is drawn too high, making it appear as though the border has been "superscripted" while the content remains where it should.

5.5.23 width

Navigator 4.x applies `width` in a very inconsistent fashion, but appears to honor it on most simple text elements and images. WinIE4/5 applies it to images and tables, but ignores it for most text elements such as P and headings. Opera 3.6, weirdly, seems to set the width of images to 100%—but this is largely an illusion, since minimizing the window and then maximizing it again will reveal correctly sized images.

5.5.25 float

`float` is one of the most complicated and hard-to-implement aspects of the entire specification. Basic floating is generally supported by all browsers, especially on images, but when the specification is closely tested, or the document structure becomes complicated, floating most often happens incorrectly, or not at all. The floating of text elements is especially inconsistent, although IE5 and Opera have cleaned up their act to a large degree, leaving WinIE4 and Nav4 the major transgressors in this respect. Authors should use `float` with some care, and thoroughly test any pages employing it with great care.

Opera 4 seems to place floated elements a little bit off from where the "ideal" place would seem to be, but in general, its support is extremely robust and can generally be counted upon.

5.5.26 clear

Like `float`, `clear` is not a simple thing to support. There is typically basic support, but as things get more complicated, browser behavior tends to break down. Thoroughly test pages using this property.

5.6.1 display

inline
Opera 3.6 almost gets `inline` right, but seems to honor the occasional carriage return as though it were a `<BR>` element, instead of plain whitespace.

5.6.3 list-style-type

none
MacNav4 displays question marks for bullets when using this value.

5.6.5 list-style-position

inside
The positioning and formatting of list-items when set to this value are a bit odd under MacIE4.

6.1 Length Units

ex

All supporting browsers (except one) appear to calculate `ex` as one-half `em`. This is arguably a reasonable approximation, but it is technically incorrect. The exception is MacIE5, which actually goes to some effort to determine the x-height of a given font.

6.3 Color Units

<keyword>

Navigator will generate a color for any apparent keyword. For example, `color: invalidValue` will yield a dark blue, and `color: inherit` (a valid declaration under CSS2) comes out as a vaguely nauseous green.

6.4 URLs

<url>

Navigator determines relative URLs with respect to the HTML document, not the stylesheet.

7

Chapter 8
CSS2 Quick Reference

The following table contains a terse description of each property in CSS2, for those times when you just need to look something up quickly but don't want to go flipping back and forth through the main part of the book. The parenthetical number following each property name refers to the section of CSS2 which describes the property. The column marked "Inh" shows whether or not the values of the given property are inherited by descendant elements.

8

Property	Values	Initial	Percentage	Inh	Applies to	Media
azimuth (19.7)	`<angle>	[[left-side	far-left	left	center-left	center	center-right	right	far-right	right-side] || behind]	leftwards	rightwards	inherit`	center	n/a	yes	all elements	aural
background (14.2.1)	`[<background-color>		<background-image>		<background-repeat>		<background-attachment>		<background-position>]	inherit`	not defined for shorthand properties	allowed for `<background-position>`	no	all elements	visual
background-attachment (14.2.1)	`scroll	fixed	inherit`	scroll	n/a	no	all elements	visual
background-color (14.2.1)	`<color>	transparent	inherit`	transparent	n/a	no	all elements	visual
background-image (14.2.1)	`<uri>	none	inherit`	none	n/a	no	all elements	visual
background-position (14.2.1)	`[[<percentage>	<length>] {1,2}	[[top	center	bottom]		[left	center	right]]]	inherit`	0% 0%	refer to the size of the box itself	no	block-level and replaced elements	visual

Property	Values	Initial	Percentage	Inh	Applies to	Media
background-repeat (14.2.1)	repeat | repeat-x | repeat-y | no-repeat | inherit	repeat	n/a	no	all elements	visual
border (8.5.4)	[<border-width> || <border-style> || <color>] | inherit	not defined for shorthand properties	n/a	no	all elements	visual
border-bottom (8.5.4)	[<border-top-width> || <border-style> || <color>] | inherit	not defined for shorthand properties	n/a	no	all elements	visual
border-bottom-color (8.5.2)	<color> | inherit	the value of the 'color' property	n/a	no	all elements	visual
border-bottom-style (8.5.3)	<border-style> | inherit	none	n/a	no	all elements	visual
border-bottom-width (8.5.1)	<border-width> | inherit	medium	n/a	no	all elements	visual
border-collapse (17.6)	collapse | separate | inherit	collapse	n/a	yes	'table' and 'inline-table' elements	visual

8

Property	Values	Initial	Percentage	Inh	Applies to	Media
border-color (8.5.2)	`<color>{1,4} | transparent | inherit`	not defined for shorthand properties	n/a	no	all elements	visual
border-left (8.5.4)	`[ <border-top-width> || <border-style> || <color> ] | inherit`	not defined for shorthand properties	n/a	no	all elements	visual
border-left-color (8.5.2)	`<color> | inherit`	the value of the 'color' property	n/a	no	all elements	visual
border-left-style (8.5.3)	`<border-style> | inherit`	none	n/a	no	all elements	visual
border-left-width (8.5.1)	`<border-width> | inherit`	medium	n/a	no	all elements	visual
border-right (8.5.4)	`[ <border-top-width> || <border-style> || <color> ] | inherit`	not defined for shorthand properties	n/a	no	all elements	visual
border-right-color (8.5.2)	`<color> | inherit`	the value of the 'color' property	n/a	no	all elements	visual

Property	Values	Initial	Percentage	Inh	Applies to	Media
border-right-style (8.5.3)	`<border-style>	inherit`	none	n/a	no	all elements	visual
border-right-width (8.5.1)	`<border-width>	inherit`	medium	n/a	no	all elements	visual
border-spacing (17.6)	`<length> <length>?	inherit`	0	n/a	yes	'table' and 'inline-table' elements	visual
border-style (8.5.3)	`<border-style>{1,4}	inherit`	not defined for shorthand properties	n/a	no	all elements	visual
border-top (8.5.4)	`[<border-top-width> || <border-style> || <color>]	inherit`	not defined for shorthand properties	n/a	no	all elements	visual
border-top-color (8.5.2)	`<color>	inherit`	the value of the 'color' property	n/a	no	all elements	visual
border-top-style (8.5.3)	`<border-style>	inherit`	none	n/a	no	all elements	visual

8

Property	Values	Initial	Percentage	Inh	Applies to	Media
border-top-width (8.5.1)	`<border-width>	inherit`	medium	n/a	no	all elements	visual
border-width (8.5.1)	`<border-width>{1,4}	inherit`	not defined for shorthand properties	n/a	no	all elements	visual
bottom (9.3.2)	`<length>	<percentage>	auto	inherit`	auto	refer to height of containing block	no	positioned elements	visual
caption-side (17.4.1)	`top	bottom	left	right	inherit`	top	n/a	yes	'table-caption' elements	visual
clear (9.5.2)	`none	left	right	both	inherit`	none	n/a	no	block-level elements	visual
clip (11.1.2)	`<shape>	auto	inherit`	auto	n/a	no	block-level and replaced elements	visual
color (14.1)	`<color>	inherit`	UA dependent	n/a	yes	all elements	visual

8

Property	Values	Initial	Percentage	Inh	Applies to	Media
content (12.2)	[<string> | <uri> | <counter> | attr(X) | open-quote | close-quote | no-open-quote | no-close-quote] + | inherit	empty string	n/a	no	:before and :after pseudo-elements	all
counter-increment (12.5)	[<identifier> <integer>?] + | none | inherit	none	n/a	no	all elements	all
counter-reset (12.5)	[<identifier> <integer>?] + | none | inherit	none	n/a	no	all elements	all
cue (19.5)	[<cue-before> || <cue-after>] | inherit	not defined for shorthand properties	n/a	no	all elements	aural
cue-after (19.5)	<uri> | none | inherit	none	n/a	no	all elements	aural
cue-before (19.5)	<uri> | none | inherit	none	n/a	no	all elements	aural
cursor (18.1)	[[<uri>,] * [auto | crosshair | default | pointer | move | e-resize | ne-resize | nw-resize | n-resize | se-resize | sw-resize | s-resize | w-resize | text | wait | help]] | inherit	auto	n/a	yes	all elements	visual, inter-active

Property	Values	Initial	Percentage	Inh	Applies to	Media
direction (9.10)	ltr | rtl | inherit	ltr	n/a	yes	all elements, but see prose	visual
display (9.2.5)	inline | block | list-item | run-in | compact | marker | table | inline-table | table-row-group | table-header-group | table-footer-group | table-row | table-column-group | table-column | table-cell | table-caption | none | inherit	inline	n/a	no	all elements	all
elevation (19.7)	<angle> | below | level | above | higher | lower | inherit	level	n/a	yes	all elements	aural
empty-cells (17.6.1)	show | hide | inherit	show	n/a	yes	'table-cell' elements	visual
float (9.5.1)	left | right | none | inherit	none	n/a	no	all but positioned elements and generated content	visual

Property	Values	Initial	Percentage	Inh	Applies to	Media
font (15.2.5)	[[<font-style> || <font-variant> || <font-weight>]? <font-size> [/<line-height>]? <font-family>] | caption | icon | menu | message-box | small-caption | status-bar | inherit	not defined for shorthand properties	allowed on 'font-size' and 'line-height'	yes	all elements	visual
font-family (15.2.2)	[[<family-name> | <generic-family>] ,]* [<family-name> | <generic-family>] | inherit	UA dependent	n/a	yes	all elements	visual
font-size (15.2.4)	<absolute-size> | <relative-size> | <length> | <percentage> | inherit	medium	refer to parent element's font size	yes	all elements	visual
font-size-adjust (15.2.4)	<number> | none | inherit	none	n/a	yes	all elements	visual
font-stretch (15.2.3)	normal | wider | narrower | ultra-condensed | extra-condensed | condensed | semi-condensed | semi-expanded | expanded | extra-expanded | ultra-expanded | inherit	normal	n/a	yes	all elements	visual

8

Property	Values	Initial	Percentage	Inh	Applies to	Media
font-style (15.2.3)	normal | italic | oblique | inherit	normal	n/a	yes	all elements	visual
font-variant (15.2.3)	normal | small-caps | inherit	normal	n/a	yes	all elements	visual
font-weight (15.2.3)	normal | bold | bolder | lighter | 100 | 200 | 300 | 400 | 500 | 600 | 700 | 800 | 900 | inherit	normal	n/a	yes	all elements	visual
height (10.5)	<length> | <percentage> | auto | inherit	auto	see prose	no	all elements except non-replaced inline elements, table columns, and column groups	visual
left (9.3.2)	<length> | <percentage> | auto | inherit	auto	refer to width of containing block	no	positioned elements	visual
letter-spacing (16.4)	normal | <length> | inherit	normal	n/a	yes	all elements	visual
line-height (10.8)	normal | <number> | <length> | <percentage> | inherit	normal	refer to the font size of the element itself	yes	all elements	visual

Property	Values	Initial	Percentage	Inh	Applies to	Media
list-style (12.6.2)	[<list-style-type> || <list-style-position> || <list-style-image>] | inherit	not defined for shorthand properties	n/a	yes	elements with 'display: list-item'	visual
list-style-image (12.6.2)	<uri> | none | inherit	none	n/a	yes	elements with 'display: list-item'	visual
list-style-position (12.6.2)	inside | outside | inherit	outside	n/a	yes	elements with 'display: list-item'	visual
list-style-type (12.6.2)	disc | circle | square | decimal | decimal-leading-zero | lower-roman | upper-roman | lower-greek | lower-alpha | lower-latin | upper-latin | upper-latin | hebrew | armenian | georgian | cjk-ideographic | hiragana | katakana | hiragana-iroha | katakana-iroha | none | inherit	disc	n/a	yes	elements with 'display: list-item'	visual
margin (8.3)	[<length> | <percentage> | auto]{1,4} | inherit	not defined for shorthand properties	refer to width of containing block	no	all elements	visual

8

Property	Values	Initial	Percentage	Inh	Applies to	Media
margin-bottom (8.3)	[<length> | <percentage> | auto] | inherit	0	refer to width of containing block	no	all elements	visual
margin-left (8.3)	[<length> | <percentage> | auto] | inherit	0	refer to width of containing block	no	all elements	visual
margin-right (8.3)	[<length> | <percentage> | auto] | inherit	0	refer to width of containing block	no	all elements	visual
margin-top (8.3)	[<length> | <percentage> | auto] | inherit	0	refer to width of containing block	no	all elements	visual
marker-offset (12.6.1)	<length> | auto | inherit	auto	n/a	no	elements with 'display: marker'	visual
marks (13.2.3)	[crop || cross] | none | inherit	none	n/a	n/a	page context	visual, paged

Property	Values	Initial	Percentage	Inh	Applies to	Media
max-height (10.7)	\<length\> | \<percentage\> | none | inherit	none	refer to height of containing block	no	all elements except non-replaced inline elements and table elements	visual
max-width (10.4)	\<length\> | \<percentage\> | none | inherit	none	refer to width of containing block	no	all elements except non-replaced inline elements and table elements	visual
min-height (10.7)	\<length\> | \<percentage\> | inherit	0	refer to height of containing block	no	all elements except non-replaced inline elements and table elements	visual

8

Property	Values	Initial	Percentage	Inh	Applies to	Media
min-width (10.4)	`<length>	<percentage>	inherit`	UA dependent	refer to width of containing block	no	all elements except non-replaced inline elements and table elements	visual
orphans (13.3.3)	`<integer>	inherit`	2	n/a	yes	block-level elements	visual, paged
outline (18.4)	`[<outline-color> || <outline-style> || <outline-width>]	inherit`	not defined for shorthand properties	n/a	no	all elements	visual, inter-active
outline-color (18.4)	`<color>	invert	inherit`	invert	n/a	no	all elements	visual, inter-active
outline-style (18.4)	`<border-style>	inherit`	none	n/a	no	all elements	visual, inter-active
outline-width (18.4)	`<border-width>	inherit`	medium	n/a	no	all elements	visual, inter-active

Property	Values	Initial	Percentage	Inh	Applies to	Media
overflow (11.1.1)	visible | hidden | scroll | auto | inherit	visible	n/a	no	block-level and replaced elements	visual
padding (8.4)	[<length> | <percentage>]{1,4} | inherit	not defined for shorthand properties	refer to width of containing block	no	all elements	visual
padding-bottom (8.4)	[<length> | <percentage>] | inherit	0	refer to width of containing block	no	all elements	visual
padding-left (8.4)	[<length> | <percentage>] | inherit	0	refer to width of containing block	no	all elements	visual
padding-right (8.4)	[<length> | <percentage>] | inherit	0	refer to width of containing block	no	all elements	visual
padding-top (8.4)	[<length> | <percentage>] | inherit	0	refer to width of containing block	no	all elements	visual
page (13.3.2)	<identifier> | auto	auto	n/a	yes	block-level elements	visual, paged

8

Property	Values	Initial	Percentage	Inh	Applies to	Media
page-break-after (13.3.1)	`auto	always	avoid	left	right	inherit`	`auto`	n/a	no	block-level elements	visual, paged
page-break-before (13.3.1)	`auto	always	avoid	left	right	inherit`	`auto`	n/a	no	block-level elements	visual, paged
page-break-inside (13.3.1)	`avoid	auto	inherit`	`auto`	n/a	yes	block-level elements	visual, paged
pause (19.4)	`[[<time>	<percentage>]{1,2}]	inherit`	UA dependent	see descriptions of 'pause-before' and 'pause-after'	no	all elements	aural
pause-after (19.4)	`<time>	<percentage>	inherit`	UA dependent	see prose	no	all elements	aural
pause-before (19.4)	`<time>	<percentage>	inherit`	UA dependent	see prose	no	all elements	aural
pitch (19.8)	`<frequency>	x-low	low	medium	high	x-high	inherit`	medium	n/a	yes	all elements	aural

Property	Values	Initial	Percentage	Inh	Applies to	Media
pitch-range (19.8)	`<number>	inherit`	50	n/a	yes	all elements	aural
play-during (19.6)	`<uri> mix? repeat?	auto	none	inherit`	auto	n/a	no	all elements	aural
position (9.3.1)	`static	relative	absolute	fixed	inherit`	static	n/a	no	all elements, but not to generated content	visual
quotes (12.4.1)	`[<string> <string>]+	none	inherit`	UA dependent	n/a	yes	all elements	visual
richness (19.8)	`<number>	inherit`	50	n/a	yes	all elements	aural
right (9.3.2)	`<length>	<percentage>	auto	inherit`	auto	refer to width of containing block	no	positioned elements	visual
size (13.2.2)	`<length>{1,2}	auto	portrait	landscape	inherit`	auto	n/a	n/a	page context	visual, paged
speak (19.3)	`normal	none	spell-out	inherit`	normal	n/a	yes	all elements	aural

8

Property	Values	Initial	Percentage	Inh	Applies to	Media
speak-header (17.7.1)	once | always | inherit	once	n/a	yes	elements that have table header information	aural
speak-numeral (19.9)	digits | continuous | inherit	continuous	n/a	yes	all elements	aural
speak-punctuation (19.9)	code | none | inherit	none	n/a	yes	all elements	aural
speech-rate (19.8)	<number> | x-slow | slow | medium | fast | x-fast | faster | slower | inherit	medium	n/a	yes	all elements	aural
stress (19.8)	<number> | inherit	50	n/a	yes	all elements	aural
table-layout (17.5.2)	auto | fixed | inherit	auto	n/a	no	'table' and 'inline-table' elements	visual
text-align (16.2)	left | right | center | justify | <string> | inherit	depends on UA and writing direction	n/a	yes	block-level elements	visual

Property	Values	Initial	Percentage	Inh	Applies to	Media
text-decoration (16.3.1)	none | [underline || overline || line-through || blink] | inherit	none	n/a	no	all elements	visual
text-indent (16.1)	<length> | <percentage> | inherit	0	refer to width of containing block	yes	block-level elements	visual
text-shadow (16.3.2)	none | [<color> || <length> <length> <length>?,]* [<color> || <length> <length> <length>?] | inherit	none	n/a	no	all elements	visual
text-transform (16.5)	capitalize | uppercase | lowercase | none | inherit	none	n/a	yes	all elements	visual
top (9.3.2)	<length> | <percentage> | auto | inherit	auto	refer to height of containing block	no	positioned elements	visual
unicode-bidi (9.10)	normal | embed | bidi-override | inherit	normal	n/a	no	all elements, but see prose	visual
vertical-align (10.8)	baseline | sub | super | top | text-top | middle | bottom | text-bottom | <percentage> | <length> | inherit	baseline	refer to the 'line-height' of the element itself	no	inline-level and 'table-cell' elements	visual
visibility (11.2)	<shape> | hidden | collapse | inherit	inherit	n/a	no	all elements	visual

8

Property	Values	Initial	Percentage	Inh	Applies to	Media
voice-family (19.8)	[[<specific-voice> | <generic-voice>],]* [<specific-voice> | <generic-voice>] | inherit	UA dependent	n/a	yes	all elements	aural
volume (19.2)	<number> | <percentage> | silent | x-soft | soft | medium | loud | x-loud | inherit	medium	refer to inherited value	yes	all elements	aural
white-space (16.6)	normal | pre | nowrap | inherit	normal	n/a	yes	block-level elements	visual
widows (13.3.3)	<integer> | inherit	2	n/a	yes	block-level elements	visual, paged
width (10.2)	<length> | <percentage> | auto | inherit	auto	refer to width of containing block	no	all elements but non-replaced inline elements, table rows, and row groups	visual

Property	Values	Initial	Percentage	Inh	Applies to	Media
word-spacing (16.4)	normal | \<length> | inherit	normal	n/a	yes	all elements	visual
z-index (9.9.1)	auto | \<integer> | inherit	auto	n/a	no	positioned elements	visual

8

Chapter 9
Useful Resources

While there isn't nearly as much information about CSS as there is about HTML, there are still a number of highly useful and very important resources available online. This chapter contains ten of the best. Please note that the omission of a certain resource does not imply that it's somehow inferior or flawed. This list simply represents the author's choices for ten highly useful sites which will provide great information covering a broad range of subjects.

Tools

CSScheck (Web Design Group)

`http://www.htmlhelp.com/tools/csscheck/`

This CSS validator is one of the best for validating your CSS. Besides performing the valuable services of catching typographical errors, malformed values and properties, as well as other problems, CSScheck explains its results with clear messages and friendly graphics. It also catches common mistakes by authors which aren't actually errors; for example, declaring a color without a background or vice versa. This is the best tool for beginning authors to check their work.

CSS Validator (World Wide Web Consortium)

`http://jigsaw.w3.org/css-validator/`

Although not nearly so user-friendly as CSScheck, this validator does have the advantage of being maintained by the W3C—the very people who wrote the CSS specification. The error and warning messages are quite terse, and the output can be a little tricky to decipher. Despite these problems, it's a very good validator and a valuable tool for the more experienced author.

Discussion Groups

Stylesheets Newsgroup (Usenet)

`news:comp.infosystems.www.authoring.stylesheets`

One of the most active CSS discussion communities, this group is a place for practical advice, passionate arguments over theory, explorations of the subtleties of the CSS specification, and everything in between. (Incidentally, due to its excessive length, the name of this group is often abbreviated to "ciwas"—pronounced *see-wass*.) New authors are encouraged to read the group's FAQs (posted twice weekly) and make use of a CSS validator before posting questions. The group charter does not prohibit discussion of style languages other than CSS, but, in practice, CSS-related messages account for well over 95% of the group's traffic. The signal-to-noise ratio is astonishingly high for a Usenet group, at least for certain definitions of "signal."

Style Discussion List (W3C)

`http://lists.w3.org/Mail/Request`

Sponsored by the World Wide Web Consortium, this list is a place to discuss the state of the CSS specification, as well as proposals for future directions in CSS. "How to" and "help me" questions are generally discouraged on this list.

Style Discussion List (HTML Writers Guild)

`http://www.hwg.org/lists/hwg-style/index.html`

The HWG maintains this list for authors who have "how to" and "help me" questions about style languages like CSS. The bulk of list subscribers seem to be real-world Web page designers, so the discussion is focused on what works and how browsers can be made to behave. As with ciwas, style languages other than CSS are open for discussion on this list, but rarely ever come up.

References

CSS Activity Page (W3C)

`http://www.w3.org/Style/CSS/`

If you're looking for the official home of CSS, this is it. In addition to providing links to the CSS specifications and drafts of new work in progress, the Activity Page provides news bulletins pointing out new tools, resources, articles, and more CSS-related stuff. You can also find links to the history of CSS, including proposals which were never adopted, pointers to other style languages, and a great deal more. If you need to get a handle on what's new and what's coming soon, this is definitely the place to go.

Style Sheets Reference Guide (Web Review)

`http://www.webreview.com/style/`

This site is home to the CSS Browser Compatibility Charts which form the basis for the chart found in Chapter 7. In addition to the charts, it contains some basic CSS information like a simple CSS FAQ and links to CSS-related articles on webreview.com. It's also maintained by the author of this book.

9

The House of Style (Western Civilisation)

`http://www.westciv.com/style_master/house/`

This site is an eclectic collection of browser compatibility information, tutorials, pre-made stylesheets, a CSS gallery, expert commentary and advice, and much more. The "good oil" articles alone make this a site worth visiting. Even more impressive, it's all the work of one man: John Allsopp, the author of Style Master. *(Note: Style Master is a commercial product. Endorsement of the House of Style does not imply endorsement of Style Master.)*

Agitprop

http://style.metrius.com/

If you've ever wondered how font sizing on the Web could be improved, you should visit this site without delay. The font articles in particular should be required reading for any Web designer, especially those who started out in the print-media world and think that the same design rules apply on the Web. Agitprop is the work of Todd Fahrner, one of the most respected CSS experts in the world.

CSS Pointers Group

http://css.nu/

This site is home to hundreds of CSS-related links, a fair number of detailed browser bug lists, articles on interesting effects and common workarounds, and much more. The CSS Pointers Group is maintained by Jan Roland Eriksson and Sue Sims, two well-known CSS gurus.

INTERNATIONAL CONTACT INFORMATION

AUSTRALIA
McGraw-Hill Book Company Australia Pty. Ltd.
TEL +61-2-9417-9899
FAX +61-2-9417-5687
http://www.mcgraw-hill.com.au
books-it_sydney@mcgraw-hill.com

CANADA
McGraw-Hill Ryerson Ltd.
TEL +905-430-5000
FAX +905-430-5020
http://www.mcgrawhill.ca

GREECE, MIDDLE EAST, NORTHERN AFRICA
McGraw-Hill Hellas
TEL +30-1-656-0990-3-4
FAX +30-1-654-5525

MEXICO (Also serving Latin America)
McGraw-Hill Interamericana Editores S.A. de C.V.
TEL +525-117-1583
FAX +525-117-1589
http://www.mcgraw-hill.com.mx
fernando_castellanos@mcgraw-hill.com

SINGAPORE (Serving Asia)
McGraw-Hill Book Company
TEL +65-863-1580
FAX +65-862-3354
http://www.mcgraw-hill.com.sg
mghasia@mcgraw-hill.com

SOUTH AFRICA
McGraw-Hill South Africa
TEL +27-11-622-7512
FAX +27-11-622-9045
robyn_swanepoel@mcgraw-hill.com

UNITED KINGDOM & EUROPE (Excluding Southern Europe)
McGraw-Hill Education Europe
TEL +44-1-628-502500
FAX +44-1-628-770224
http://www.mcgraw-hill.co.uk
computing_neurope@mcgraw-hill.com

ALL OTHER INQUIRIES Contact:
Osborne/McGraw-Hill
TEL +1-510-549-6600
FAX +1-510-883-7600
http://www.osborne.com
omg_international@mcgraw-hill.com